# THE BOOK:
# THE TANGIBLE EVIDENCE OF THE HOLY SPIRIT

Discover The Power To Propel You From
Minimum To Maximum Capacity

DR. CHARLES KARUKU

# THE BOOK: THE TANGIBLE EVIDENCE OF THE HOLY SPIRIT.

ISBN - 13: 9781797430089

# TABLE OF CONTENTS

# OBJECTIVE OF THE BOOK

Whenever you see the glory, know there's a story. This book is written from my heart. It is my life in print. It is the story behind the glory that has propelled me from common to uncommon levels. However, this book is more than just that. It is not only a story of a young, peasant boy that God picked from the jungles of Africa and put him on the frontline of an international ministry. This is a story of all people who look like David, the shepherd boy. When God told Samuel to go to the house of Jesse and anoint the next King of Israel, David was a nobody. He was not even invited to the anointing ceremony. His father considered only his well-built-tall and handsome brothers. But God looks into the inside and not the outside. David had to be summoned from the bush to come and receive the anointing to become the greatest King that Israel has ever had. As you read this book, the Lord will summon you from whatever (bush), condition or position you are in. He will anoint you with the power of the Holy Spirit. That power will transform you. You shall become a history maker in the land.

Those kinds of things don't just happen. Behind every glory, there is a story. There are process and protocols that are necessary to make such a shift. We should never forget that it was the power of the Holy Spirit that came upon David. That power moved him from being a shepherd boy in the jungles of the Middle East to being on the top of the world stage. This book explores the dynamics and inner workings of the Holy Spirit.

The easy-to-read format of this book makes it very down to earth. Also, the juxtaposition of theological exposition and my life story makes it easy to relate to. It is my goal to inspire, motivate, break mindsets and even challenge you to reach out to the Holy Spirit. You too can embrace the tangible evidence of the Holy Spirit to enable you to move from common to uncommon levels.

If I do that, this book will have served its purpose. The real goal of this book is to set you apart and get you filled with so much power of the Holy Spirit. You will operate in the power of the New Testament Spirit-Filled Christian. I have included a powerful chapter of fire prayers. The anointing you will receive through reading this book will empower you to intercede with the supernatural power of the Holy Spirit. Your prayer life will never be the same again. It will empower your prayers to have uncommon answers. You will see supernatural results. Your world will begin to shift into a territory of favor and victory that you have never seen. Your stolen goods shall return to you in hundred folds.

Oh , how I ask that the prayer of my grandfather Joshua would be answered in you like it has been in me. He prayed that God would raise a generation of true witnesses full of the Spirit of God and boldness . That they would testify to this world of the wonders of our God. May your life , testimony , and story be a sign and wonder of the tangible evidence of the Holy Spirit. May you be a witness ( one who has a first-hand experience of something). God is still look - ing for people that He can manifest Himself through.

You will no longer be talking about the Holy Spirit as a distant subject. Your life, your walk, and your testimony will become THE TANGIBLE EVIDENCE OF THE HOLY SPIRIT. He will move you from common to uncommon levels.

Welcome to a new dimension.

# SPECIAL QUOTES

*"Ye shall receive power after that the Holy Ghost is come upon you"* (Jesus Christ)

*"When the Holy Ghost is on somebody, He shows up in their life by manifesting the power and tangible evidence of His presence. We have the same Spirit that was in Jesus, the same manifestations, the same fruit, and the same gifts. We have not been given another spirit."* (Dr. Charles Karuku)

# SPECIAL NOTES

I wrote this book from my heart and in my own unique style. I just wanted to make sure it comes out as a personal moment of having a heart-to-heart talk with you. I wanted the book to reflect the feel of that personal touch that should not be lost through print. This is the best I can do in terms of opening my heart and sharing from the deep recess of what the Lord has laid on my life after many years of walking with the tangible evidence of the Holy Spirit.

Finally, for those who have asked me to share my testimony, your wish has been granted. I have also wanted to honor those who have impacted me on my journey. Not that I have arrived. I am still learning. However, I realize there is a lot of things to share after being on the frontline of healing ministry since 1991. There is a reason why God has been moving with miracles in such a large scale. In all my travels to the nations, I keep seeing the tumors disappear, the lame walk, the blind see, and the deaf hear as people come to Jesus in droves. There has to be a story behind the glory. It is time that I share the secret of that glory.

# PRELUDE

From the Upper room to the Azusa Street revival and to the modern revivals, the Lord has not stopped covering the earth with His glory. Such mighty Holy Spirit outpourings have always resulted into societal transformations that are way beyond what natural social, economic or political revolutions can do. We have heard of cities and towns where prisons, brothels, bars and houses of ill repute have been shut down as people turn to God. It has been reported in such places of how local police officers have had no incidences as people no longer get involved in crime. We have heard of places where business, media, and political leaders have welcomed God into their arena and seen major moves of the Holy Spirit unfold. But all these societal transformations begin with one heart at a time. They ignite and transform one person at a time, and then a group of transformed people comes together to transform the culture. It reveals the power of one. When one person gets the real encounter with the Holy Spirit, they become the salt and light of the world around them. It is true that politicians and governments cannot change the world for good without God. That is why the church must experience the tangible evidence of the Holy Spirit. We cannot legislate morality. Unless God gives us a real encounter for genuine personal transformation, there is no hope for a real change no matter what kind of policies the governments adopt.

So, what is the tangible evidence of the Holy Spirit? We have traditionally looked at speaking in tongues as the initial evidence of the Holy Spirit baptism. The Lord impressed on my heart to address some issues that I honestly feel have been misunderstood or misrepresented altogether. Is tongues the only evidence? If so, then why is it that a person can speak in tongues and still have no love? (1 Cor 13:1). If tongues were the only evidence, then why is it that some people who speak in tongues lead such a defeated life? Does that mean tongues do not matter? Absolutely not!

This book seeks to establish the case that Jesus promised the church power and not just tongues. The early church received power not just tongues. That is what changed their world. They had no money, no TVs, no advanced technology and even no bibles. Yet, with all those limitations, they were able to use the power of the Holy Spirit to change their world. This book seeks to bring out the same Spirit and experiences that the early church had. We are not trying to go back to the book of Acts. For those who are good students of the Bible, you realize the church of Acts was not perfect. It had its flaws just like any other move of God that is released through people of flesh and blood. God wants to restore His initial plan and intention for His people to walk in greater power and authority in the fullness of the Holy Spirit. This book takes us on a journey that unpacks step-by-step, what it means to demonstrate such tangible evidence.

It all began with a quest that took me over a decade and a half. I began to want what Peter had. After a careful biblical study and prayer, God performed His word in my life just as He promised to do. This experience was very revolutionary. It lifted me from the jungles of Africa and propelled me to the frontline of healing ministry to my generation. That is what pushed me to write this book. I have seen countless miracles as a result and traveled to multiple nations blazing the trail with a ministry of healing, deliverance, signs and wonders. After having a tangible personal evidence, it became apparent that if I can have it today, anybody and everybody should have access to it also. This book is for those who are hungry for the real genuine power and evidence of the Holy Spirit. Do you want the power of God? Do you want a deeper and more vital relationship with the Holy Spirit? Do you want the same Holy Spirit that filled Jesus with power? Do you want to operate in the gifts of the Holy Spirit and bear His fruits? If that is you, then your day of power has arrived. In this book, I also define terms like being filled and being baptized with the Holy Spirit. I will explain the two kinds of tongues and why you need to clear the fog of confusion and get ahead in your understanding of the Holy Spirit.

When the Lord laid on my heart to write this book, my first concern was that there are enough books on this subject already. However, after a further review of many books and inputs on the subject of the Holy Spirit, I found out that there is a lot that has not yet been covered. I believe that there is something for me to contribute to the body of Christ. I have read books and materials that claim that the gifts of the Spirit have ceased. Also, I have found out that most of the people who write those books do it out of lack of tangible evidence of the working of the Holy Spirit in their lives. I felt like the best person to talk about the Holy Spirit is the one that would do it out of personal first-hand experience. It is hard for someone who does not have the evidence of the gifts and encounters of the Holy Spirit to be able to speak confidently on the matter. I don't claim to know it all. I am still a student of the Holy Spirit. When I think I know Him, I just find how little I know of Him. It makes me want more. But in this book, I try to build a case of how the biblical claims of the Holy Spirit can also become our personal experiences today, here and now. I remove the limits and restrictions of theological leanings and biases so that the Bible can come alive. It is my prayer that the words of the Bible would jump out of its pages and become a living, tangible evidence that we can live out for all to see.

As my papa, Dr. Morris Celurro says, "God will not use anybody until He gives them an experience." May this be your experience that gives you tangible evidence to move forward with the greater power of the Holy Spirit.

Everlastingly at it,
Dr. Charles
May 2012.

# DEDICATION

To my family, the most Godly people you can find. You are a solid rock in my life . Your tenacity and steadfastness is like wind underneath my wings. I love you now even more than words can express.

My mom, Miriam who taught me how to pray and have faith in God. Her tenacity and unshakable faith have given me a resilience that is priceless. It's become what I'm known for around the world.

My dad whom I never met, but everyone tells me I resemble him in so many good ways. I can feel the mantle of my father and the redemption of his legacy.

I also dedicate this work to my grandfather Joshua (of blessed memory) whose prophetic prayers have been answered through me. His legacy has given me something to pass on to the next generation.

My children Miriam, Israel, Jehu, Jemimah, and Phoebe. You're my ultimate dream come true. I've always wanted to inspire you. May this book be a way for me to give you broad shoulders on which to stand tall and aim higher. You're my legacy, and I love you dearly.

# CHAPTER 1

# THE PERSON
# OF THE HOLY SPIRIT

The Holy Spirit is not a force. He is a person. He has emotions, feelings, desires, a personality and can speak. He is the third person of the Godhead. The Bible clearly helps us to understand the Holy Spirit as a person. He reveals Himself in two distinct dispensations. He is the same Spirit but in different manifestations.

Understanding the Holy Spirit is critical to our ability to host Him better. We are able to know His nature, His likes, and dislikes. The Holy Spirit is so humble and very meek. He never allows Himself to strive with men. He stays away from anything that is not fluid. Many people have quenched or grieved the Holy Spirit for lack of understanding of His protocols. He is not pushy. He has so much protocol and loves to be invited. His personality requires that we be very sensitive to Him. He also requires of us to let Him give us the lead in everything. When He is invited, the Holy Spirit desires to take charge. That is when He feels free to have His way and also to lead and speak. That level of cooperation and partnership requires that we be in a position to interact with Him in a very intimate way. He knows our motives and is very gracious. He even gives us multiple chances to make mistakes and learn. When we have a teachable spirit, He will unfold things to us that will take us places we have never known before. The depth of knowing Him are beyond searching.

The most awesome thing is that He is just a breath away. He can come into us in just a twinkling of an eye. He loves to be unleashed to work on our behalf.

Just ask Him to come right now and lead you into deeper dimensions of intimacy as you journey through this book.

## THE THREE DISPENSATIONS OF THE HOLY SPIRIT.

### THE FIRST DISPENSATION- THE VISITATION.

The Bible gives us multiple promises of the Holy Spirit. In the book of Genesis 1:2 we see the first mention of the Holy Spirit hovering over the space of the water.

'The earth was without form and an empty waste, and darkness was upon the face of the very great deep. The Spirit of God was moving (hovering, brooding) over the face of the waters.' (AMP)

In Genesis 1:26 we see the second mention of the Holy Spirit as the Godhead.

'God said, Let Us [Father, Son, and Holy Spirit] make mankind in Our image, after Our likeness, and let them have complete authority over the fish of the sea, the birds of the air, the [tame] beasts, and over all of the earth, and over everything that creeps upon the earth.'

The Holy Spirit is promised to us as the image and likeness of God. We are not complete until we receive the image and likeness of God through the Holy Spirit. We are still without form and void until the Holy Spirit comes into our lives. The Holy Spirit gives form and life to us. We are nothing without Him. The Bible describes people without the Holy Spirit as spiritually dead. Allow the Holy Spirit to form you into the kind of person God wants you to be.

Different people in the Bible promised or prophesied the coming of the Holy Spirit. Genesis 8:6–12 outlines the two dispensations of the Holy Spirit.

'At the end of [another] forty days Noah opened a window of the ark which he had made. And sent forth a raven, which kept going to and fro until the waters were dried up from the land. Then he sent forth a dove to see if the waters had decreased from the surface of the ground. But the dove found no resting-place on which to roost, and she returned to him to the ark, for the waters were [yet] on the face of the whole land. So he put forth his hand and drew her to him into the ark. He waited another seven days and again sent forth the dove out of the ark. And the dove came back to him in the evening, and behold, in her mouth was a newly sprouted and freshly plucked olive leaf! So Noah knew that the waters had subsided from the land. Then he waited another seven days and sent forth the dove, but she did not return to him anymore.'

After the flood, Noah took a dove which is a symbol of the Holy Spirit (This symbol will be discussed in details under the topic of "The Symbols of the Holy Spirit). Noah stands for God while the dove stands for the Holy Spirit. Noah released the dove to go from the ark to see if the waters had subsided from the face of the earth. The dove found no resting place for her foot, so she returned to the ark. So he put out his hand and took her and drew her into the ark to himself.

'Then he sent forth a dove to see if the waters had decreased from the surface of the ground. But the dove found no resting-place on which to roost, and she returned to him to the ark, for the waters were [yet] on the face of the whole land. So he put forth his hand and drew her to him into the ark' (Genesis 8:8-9).

This was a prophetic symbol of the dispensations of the Holy Spirit. In the Old Testament dispensation, God sent the Holy Spirit temporarily for the purpose of releasing prophetic decrees into the earth. The Holy Spirit was never allowed to settle in the earth, but would only come and go after fulfilling His mission. Furthermore, only the kings, priests and prophets had the Holy Spirit. The purpose of the Holy Spirit was to help them temporarily in their calling. He helped them carry out the assignments of the Lord. As soon as that assignment was complete, the Holy Spirit would lift until the next assignment. The first dispensation of the Holy Spirit can rightly be called the visitation dispensation. Nobody was able to host the Holy Spirit or build a permanent abode for Him. You have to bear in mind that the Old Testament dispensation did not have salvation as we know it today. There was no finished work of Jesus on the cross to deal with sin. Even those who walked with the Lord did not enjoy the access we have today through Jesus Christ. They envied the generation of the last days when God would pour out His Spirit upon ALL flesh (Joel 2:28). We should be very thankful  that we are no longer  living  in the dispensation of the visitations of the Lord. We are in the second dispensation of habitation. Praise the Lord!

## *THE SECOND DISPENSATION-THE HABITATION.*

Noah waited another seven days and sent the dove out of the ark.

> 'He waited another seven days and again sent forth the dove out of the ark. And the dove came back to him in the evening, and behold, in her mouth was a newly sprouted and freshly plucked olive leaf! So Noah knew that the waters had subsided from the land. Then he waited another seven days and sent forth the dove, but she did not return to him any more' (Genesis 8:10-12).

The dove came back that night with a freshly plucked olive leaf in her mouth. Noah knew that the waters had abated from the earth. He waited another seven days and sent out the dove, and it did not return to him anymore. This was a type of the beginning of the second dispensation of the Holy Spirit which came with Jesus in the New Testament. It was a habitation dispensation. During this second dispensation, God promises to release the Holy Spirit into the earth to come and live and dwell among us. Joel prophesied about this dispensation and calls it an outpouring of the Spirit upon all flesh.

> 'And afterward I will pour out My Spirit upon all flesh; and your sons and your daughters shall prophesy, your old men shall dream dreams, your young men shall see visions' (Joel 2:28).

We are living in this new dispensation of the Holy Spirit. This book will deal mainly with the second dispensation of the Holy Spirit. There is a need to know how to host the Holy Spirit not as a guest but as a friend. He is no longer coming for a short visitation. He is here to stay for the long haul. We better know how to get along with Him.

## THE THIRD DISPENSATION.

Paul, however, prophesies of a third dispensation of the Holy Spirit. In the book of 2Thes 2:1-9, Paul describes the Holy Spirit as the one that restrains the antichrist from being fully revealed in the earth.

'But relative to the coming of our Lord Jesus Christ (the Messiah) and our gathering together to [meet] Him, we beg you, brethren, Not to allow your minds to be quickly unsettled or disturbed or kept excited or alarmed, whether it be by some [pretended] revelation of [the] Spirit or by word or by letter [alleged to be] from us, to the effect that the day of the Lord has [already] arrived and is here. Let no one deceive or beguile you in any way, for that day will not come except the apostasy comes first [unless the predicted great falling away of those who have professed to be Christians has come], and the man of lawlessness (sin) is revealed, who is the son of doom (of perdition), Who opposes and exalts himself so proudly and insolently against and over all that is called God or that is worshiped, [even to his actually] taking his seat in the temple of God, proclaiming that he himself is God. Do you not recollect that when I was still with you, I told you these things? And now you know what is restraining him [from being revealed at this time]; it is so that he may be manifested (revealed) in his own [appointed] time. For the mystery of lawlessness (that hidden principle of rebellion against constituted authority) is already at work in the world, [but it is] restrained only until he who restrains is taken out of the way. And then the lawless one (the antichrist) will be revealed, and the Lord Jesus will slay him with the breath of His mouth and bring him to an end by His appearing at His coming. The coming [of the lawless one, the antichrist] is through the activity and working of Satan and will be attended by great power and with all sorts of [pretended] miracles and signs and delusive marvels--[all of them] lying wonders.'

In verse 8, Paul writes of a dispensation when the Holy Spirit will be removed from the earth. This is the time that marks the end of the current dispensation of grace as we know it. The church shall be taken away suddenly at a time we call the rapture of the church. (The catching away of the church when Jesus comes back for her bride). Then after that event, the world will see the full manifestation of the person and the spirit of the antichrist. Those words suggest that there is a third dispensation of the Holy Spirit that is yet to come. The Holy Spirit will be the main player in the event of the rapture of the church. He will be the one who shall present the church as the bride with no spots or wrinkles. His work of perfecting the saints will have been completed. The rapture of the church will be the day that completes the assignment of the Holy Spirit on the earth. It will mark the beginning of the third dispensation where the Holy Spirit returns back to God with the words, "mission accomplished." I would never want to be in this world one moment after the Holy Spirit completes His earthly mission. That is why I believe that no truly-blood-bought-child of God will be left behind in the earth when the Holy Spirit completes His mission. Paul tells us that the mission of the Holy Spirit is to perfect the saints and prepare the church to be a spotless bride with no wrinkles.

'that He might sanctify and cleanse her with the washing of water by the word, that He might present her to Himself a glorious church, not having spot or wrinkle or any such thing, but that she should be holy and without blemish.' Ephesians 5:26-27 NKJV

# CHAPTER 2

# THE PROMISES
# OF THE HOLY SPIRIT.

## THE PROMISE OF JOEL

Joel 2:28-31:

Joel prophesied the outpouring on all flesh. The Holy Spirit would be poured out to sons, daughters, old men, young men, men servants and maid servants. This is a complete departure from the Old Testament dispensation where the Holy Spirit was only restricted to the priests, prophets, and kings. Joel prophesied a landmark breakthrough in God's desire to make the Holy Spirit accessible to everybody. What was previously exclusive in the Old Testament becomes inclusive in the New Testament. Joel opens the door to the new era of total unlimited access to the Holy Spirit! This is one benefit of the finished work of Jesus on the cross. The way is now open for all. We are living in the day of the fulfillment of this prophecy. Joel promises that when the Holy Spirit is poured out dreams, visions, prophecy, signs, and wonders are going to take place as a result. He also promised that this outpouring will be before the coming of the great and terrible day of the Lord.

Joel described this time when all people of all gender, young and old, will be filled with the Holy Spirit. There will also be a display of the Holy Spirit power as a sign that the end is near.

'And afterward I will pour out My Spirit upon all flesh; and your sons and your daughters shall prophesy, your old men shall dream dreams, your young men shall see visions. Even upon the menservants and upon the maidservants in those days will I pour out My Spirit. And I will show signs and wonders in the heavens, and on the earth, blood and fire and columns of smoke. The sun shall be turned to darkness and the moon to blood before the great and terrible day of the Lord comes' (Joel 2:28-31).

## THE PETER'S PROMISE.

Joel's prophecy was fulfilled in Acts 2 after the outpouring of the Holy Spirit on the day of Pentecost. Peter responded with a biblical explanation of what had just occurred. In Acts 2:16 Peter recounts the prophecy of Joel 2:28.

'But [instead] this is [the beginning of] what was spoken through the prophet Joel.' It is biblically sound to conclude that the outpouring of the Holy Spirit began in the upper room and continues until the second coming of the Lord.

Peter also explained how this outpouring will continue to all the generations that will come. In Acts 2:38-39 Peter promises the Holy Spirit to our children, to all who are far away and to as many the Lord will call.

> 'And Peter answered them, Repent (change your views and purpose to accept the will of God in your inner selves instead of rejecting it) and be baptized, every one of you, in the name of Jesus Christ for the forgiveness of and release from your sins; and you shall receive the gift of the Holy Spirit. For the promise [of the Holy Spirit] is to and for you and your children, and to and for all that are far away, [even] to and for as many, as the Lord, our God invites and bids to come to Himself.'

This means that all the future generations of believers have access to the same outpouring that was promised by Joel. According to these promises, the releasing of the Holy Spirit shall not cease until the coming of the Lord. This prophecy is very revolutionary.

Peter describes the outpouring of the Holy Spirit as times of refreshing from the presence of the Lord. That outpouring of the refreshing is promised to those who repent.

'So repent (change your mind and purpose); turn around and return [to God], that your sins may be erased (blotted out, wiped clean), that times of refreshing (of recovering from the effects of heat, of reviving with fresh air) may come from the presence of the Lord; And that He may send [to you] the Christ (the Messiah), Who before was designated and appointed for you--even Jesus, Whom heaven must receive [and retain] until the time for the complete restoration of all that God spoke by the mouth of all His holy prophets for ages past [from the most ancient time in the memory of man]' (Act 3:19-21).

## PROMISE GIVEN BY JOHN THE BAPTIST.

John the Baptist describes himself as a voice crying out in the wilderness to prepare the way of the Lord. He also prophesied that Jesus would baptize with the Holy Spirit and fire.

'1 indeed baptize you in (with) water because of repentance [that is, because of your changing your minds for the better, heartily amending your ways, with abhorrence of your past sins]. But He Who is coming after me is mightier than I, Whose sandals I am not worthy or fit to take off or carry; He will baptize you with the Holy Spirit and with fire' (Matthew 3:11).

John the Baptist comes with the spirit of Elijah. He was an intercessor who spent time in the wilderness praying, fasting and waiting for the fulfillment of the promise of the

Messiah. Through his intercession, Jesus was preserved until the day of His unveiling. John did the unveiling. He described Jesus as the baptizer in the Holy Spirit and fire. This is the simple answer to the question of who baptizes believers with the Holy Spirit? Jesus saves and also baptizes with the Holy Spirit and fire. This is part of His ministry to a believer. He will do it just like He promised His disciples while they waited in the upper room (Acts 2:1-4).

## PROMISE ACCORDING TO JESUS

Jesus Himself spoke very widely of the coming of the Holy Spirit. In the book of Mark 16:17, He promised that all those who believed shall speak in other tongues.

> 'And these attesting signs will accompany those who believe: in My name, they will drive out demons; they will speak in new languages.'

This was a promise that points to Acts 2:1-4 where all those who gathered in the upper room were filled with the Holy Spirit and spoke in tongues.

> 'And when the day of Pentecost had fully come, they were all assembled together in one place, When suddenly there came a sound from heaven like the rushing of a violent tempest blast, and it filled the whole house in which they were sitting. And there appeared to them tongues resembling fire, which were separated and distributed and which settled on each one of them. And

they were all filled (diffused throughout their souls) with the Holy Spirit and began to speak in other (different, foreign) languages (tongues), as the Spirit kept giving them clear and loud expression [in each tongue in appropriate words].'

Jesus promised the releasing of the power of the Holy Spirit from on high. This again points to the upper room experience of Acts 2:1-4 where the Holy Spirit was released from heaven as the 120 waited.

'And behold, I will send forth upon you what My Father has promised; but remain in the city [Jerusalem] until you are clothed with power from on high' (Luke 24:49).

The book of John is full of promises from Jesus. John 7:38-39 gives a promise of the Holy Spirit coming to dwell inside of us.

'He who believes in Me [who cleaves to and trusts in and relies on Me] as the Scripture has said, From his innermost being shall flow [continuously] springs and rivers of living water. But He was speaking here of the Spirit, Whom those who believed (trusted, had faith) in Him were afterward to receive. For the [Holy] Spirit had not yet been given, because Jesus was not yet glorified (raised to honor).'

Jesus explained that when the Holy Spirit comes, He will flow out of our belly like a river. The waters that will come out of that river will be living waters. This is what Ezekiel saw in his prophetic vision:

'Then he [my guide] brought me again to the door of the house [of the Lord--the temple], and behold, waters issued out from under the threshold of the temple toward the east, for the front of the temple was toward the east; and the waters came down from under, from the right side of the temple, on the south side of the altar. Then he brought me out by way of the north gate and led me around outside to the outer gate by the way that faces east, and behold, waters were running out on the right side. And when the man went on eastward with the measuring line in his hand, he measured a thousand cubits, and he caused me to pass through the waters, waters that were ankle-deep. Again he measured a thousand cubits and caused me to pass through the waters, waters that reached to the knees. Again he measured a thousand cubits and caused me to pass through the waters, waters that reached to the loins. Afterward, he measured a thousand, and it was a river that I could not pass through, for the waters had risen, waters to swim in, a river that could not be passed over or through. And he said to me, Son of man, have you seen this? Then he led me and caused me to return to the bank of the river. Now when I had returned, behold, on the bank of the river were very many trees on the one side and on the other. Then he said to me, These waters pour out toward the eastern region and go down into the Arabah (the Jordan

Valley) and on into the Dead Sea. And when they shall enter into the sea [the sea of putrid waters], the waters shall be healed and made fresh. And wherever the double river shall go, every living creature which swarms shall live. And there shall be a very great number of fish, because these waters go there that [the waters of the sea] may be healed and made fresh; and everything shall live wherever the river goes. The fishermen shall stand on [the banks of the Dead Sea]; from En-pedi even to En-eglaim shall be a place to spread nets; their fish shall be of very many kinds, as the fish of the Great or Mediterranean Sea. But its swamps and marshes will not become wholesome for animal life; they shall [as the river subsides] be left encrusted with salt and given over to it. And on the banks of the river on both its sides, there shall grow all kinds of trees for food; their leaf shall not fade nor shall their fruit fail [to meet the demand]. Each tree shall bring forth new fruit every month, [these supernatural qualities being] because their waters came from out of the sanctuary. And their fruit shall be for food and their leaves for healing' (Ezekiel 47:1-12).

This vision of Ezekiel illustrates the flow of life through the outpouring of the Holy Spirit. Ezekiel described this as healing waters (Ezekiel 47: 8). He also described them as life-giving waters. Everything will live wherever the river goes (Ezekiel 47:9). The waters are described as fruit giving waters where there is no barrenness but rather fruitfulness and growth (Ezekiel 47:12). Jesus explained that water means the Holy Spirit. We are living in the day of the fulfillment of this promise of Ezekiel. God is pouring out His spirit for the purpose of refreshing and giving of life to us His children.

In Acts 1:4-5 there is the promise of the Father in regard to the Holy Spirit.

> 'And while being in their company and eating with them, He commanded them not to leave Jerusalem but to wait for what the Father had promised, Of which [He said] you have heard Me speak. For John baptized with water, but not many days from now you shall be baptized with (placed in, introduced into) the Holy Spirit.'

Jesus commanded the disciples to wait for this promise before they could depart from Jerusalem.

> "And I will ask the Father, and He will give you another Comforter (Counselor, Helper, Intercessor, Advocate, Strengthener, and Standby), that He may remain with you forever. The Spirit of Truth, Whom the world cannot receive (welcome, take to its heart) because it does not see Him or know and recognize Him. But you know and recognize Him, for He lives with you [constantly] and will be in you' (John 14:16-17).

> 'But the Comforter (Counselor, Helper, Intercessor, Advocate, Strengthener, Standby), the Holy Spirit, Whom

the Father will send in My name [in My place, to represent Me and act on My behalf], He will teach you all things. And He will cause you to recall (will remind you of, bring to your remembrance) everything I have told you' (John 14:26).

Jesus also promised that the power of the Holy Spirit would come upon them. The Holy Spirit will not only dwell in the inside but also in the outside. That is why this is a baptism. It's an inside and also an outside job of Holy Spirit outpouring.

'He said to them, It is not for you to become acquainted with and know what time brings [the things and events of time and their definite periods] or fixed years and seasons (their critical niche in time), which the Father has appointed (fixed and reserved) by His own choice and authority and personal power' ( Acts 1:7).

In John 14:16-20 Jesus gave the following four promises:

1. He will pray to the Father for us to get the Holy Spirit as a helper that abides with us forever.
2. The Holy Spirit will come to bring truth, to dwell and be in us.
3. That we will not be left orphans. The Holy Spirit will come to be a companion and a comforter helping us along.
4. The Holy Spirit will manifest Himself to us.

'And I will ask the Father, and He will give you another Comforter (Counselor, Helper, Intercessor, Advocate, Strengthener, and Standby), that He may remain with you forever-The Spirit of Truth, Whom the world cannot receive (welcome, take to its heart), because it does not see Him or know and recognize Him. But you know and recognize Him, for He lives with you [constantly] and will be in you. I will not leave you as orphans [comfortless, desolate, bereaved, forlorn, helpless]; I will come [back] to you. Just a little while now, and the world will not see Me anymore, but you will see Me; because I live, you will live also. At that time [when that day comes] you will know [for yourselves] that I am in My Father, and you [are] in Me, and I [am] in you."

Jesus said that We (Father, Son, Holy Spirit) will come and make a home inside of us. 'Jesus answered, If a person [really] loves Me, he will keep My word [obey My teaching]; and My Father will love him, and We will come to him and make Our home (abode, special dwelling place) with him' (John 14:23).

Jesus promised that the Father will send the Holy Spirit in His name. 'But the Comforter (Counselor, Helper, Intercessor, Advocate, Strengthener, Standby), the Holy Spirit, Whom the Father will send in My name [in My place, to represent Me and act on My behalf], He will teach you all things. And He will cause you to recall (will remind you of, bring to your remembrance) everything I have told you' (John 14:26).

Jesus said that it is to our advantage that He goes away so that He can send the Holy Spirit to us.

> 'However, I am telling you nothing but the truth when I say it is profitable (good, expedient, advantageous) for you that I go away. Because if I do not go away, the Comforter (Counselor, Helper, Advocate, Intercessor, Strengthener, Standby) will not come to you [into close fellowship with you]; but if I go away, I will send Him to you [to be in close fellowship with you]' (John 16:7).

His ascension fulfilled this promise. After his departure in Acts 2, it took only ten days for the Holy Spirit to be released.

## PROMISES OF ISAIAH

Isaiah 44:3 prophesied of the outpouring of the Holy Spirit on the future descendants. This clearly points to the church which is also called the seed of Abraham.

> 'For I will pour water upon him who is thirsty, and floods upon the dry ground. I will pour My Spirit upon your offspring, and My blessing upon your descendants.'

Isaiah prophesied of the refreshing to come as God speaks to his people with stammering lips.

'No, but [the Lord will teach the rebels in a more humiliating way] by men with stammering lips and another tongue will He speak to this people [says Isaiah, and teach them His lessons]. To these [complaining Jews the Lord] had said, This is the true rest [the way to true comfort and happiness] that you shall give to the weary, and, This is the [true] refreshing--yet they would not listen [to His teaching]' (Isaiah 28:11-12).

This points to the outpouring of the Holy Spirit, speaking in other tongues and the refreshing thereof.

Isaiah 41:18 promised to open rivers in high places and fountains in the midst of the valley. He promised to make the wilderness a pool of water and the dry places spring of water. This repeated mention of water points to the outpouring of the Holy Spirit.

'I will open rivers on the bare heights, and fountains in the midst of the valleys; I will make the wilderness a pool of water, and the dry land springs of water.'

## CONCLUSION OF THE PROMISES

One of the reasons why I wrote this book is to bring the subject of the Holy Spirit from the mystical realm to a simple concept that is easy for all to access. It took me over three years to receive the Holy Spirit. I spent all those years crying out to God to fill me. I was so disappointed and angry with myself and God for not doing it for me. After many disappointing and desperate moments, I finally found the secret. One day, while in the university, I stumbled on a book by Dr. John Osteen. It was a very tiny book on the Holy Spirit. I don't know if I really read the book. I devoured the book and hung on every word and promise. Within three days, I was gloriously baptized with the Holy Spirit. That was August 1st, 1993. I finally found out that it was never supposed to be that complicated. However, lack of clear and concise teaching on this subject mystifies it. My goal is to make this a low hanging fruit for all ages and races to partake. It's my desire that you will get to know the Holy Spirit more intimately as I help you to study the scriptures in their simplicity.

We need to settle the fact that God will never lie. His word is always true. Then from there, we can begin to move from doubt to persistent faith in His word. Lack of knowledge is an open door for the enemy to rob us of what God has promised. It is amazing what difference a simple adjustment and alignment to the truth can do.

Many times when we fail to obtain the promises of God, we blame Him in frustration. Other times we condemn ourselves. Satan is the accuser of brethren. He uses those moments to accuse. He accuses God to us of not answering our prayer. He (the enemy) lies to us not to believe God's word again. Satan also accuses us of not being good enough. He may even accuse the word of God for not being truthful.

When we face insurmountable frustrations, it is so easy to believe the enemy's lies. Let me state this very clearly: In most cases, there may not necessarily be anything sinful in our lives. Many times, it is a very simple truth that we have not grasped properly. We need to settle the fact that God will never lie. His word is always true. Then from there, we can begin to move from doubt to persistent faith in His word. Lack of knowledge is an open door for the enemy to rob us of what God has promised. It is amazing what difference a simple adjustment and alignment to the truth can do. When a bone is dislocated, it can make the back or neck to be completely stiff and impossible to move. When you go to a physical therapist, within five minutes of a simple adjust-ment, everything can come back to alignment, and full movement is restored. God's truth works like that also. When we realign ourselves with His divine order, the flow of the promises of God comes automatically. What seemed too hard to achieve becomes very easy. Sometimes it's not more pushing and striving. Sometimes it is a simple adjustment. For me, that simple adjustment is what I lacked. When I got it, I entered into the flow of the Holy Spirit, and I have never looked back.

Don't allow the enemy to condemn and cause you to miss out on the promise of the outpouring of the Holy Spirit. Do not also fall into the temptation to do a bunch of works to fulfill God's promises in your own strength. I can remember the many times I went into prayer, fasting and begging God to fill me with the Holy Spirit. What I did not understand was that a free gift from the Lord does not come with conditions of more fasting and prayer and begging. It is supposed to be received with a thankful heart. God has already made a true promise to those that are of the household of faith. It is up to us to learn how to receive. If I promise my children $5.00 gift, they have no need of going into fasting, prayer and begging to receive it. All they should do is know that I am faithful to my promise and then they can come to receive the gift with a thankful heart. Once they approach my presence, all they need to do is to make me aware that they are there to receive what I promised. Then my work is to reach down into my pocket and give them the money as I promised. Once they receive, they are supposed to thank me and then walk away rejoicing. That was the simple lesson I learned after three years of struggling. I needed to learn how to receive from God. I did not need to earn what has already been earned and made available through the finished work of a Jesus on the cross. I needed to just receive. Since that time, I have been convinced that the baptism in the Holy Spirit is a blood-bought birthright of all the believers. It should be received as easy and as quickly as salvation. There is no reason to wait for weeks or months. It should be possible to receive even in a matter of days! In fact, it took the disciples only ten days to receive after Jesus told them to wait. In many cases, people have received the Holy Spirit instantly after getting born again. That is how present and powerful God's promises are. In our ministry since 1994, many times we see people get saved and receive the baptism in the Holy Ghost at the same time.

Back to my life testimony; It became very clear that the reason why we perish is due to lack of knowledge. One day I got a hold of a simple book on how to receive the Holy Spirit. I read and devoured it several times until everything went deep into my spirit. Within a few days of reading the book, at two O'clock, in the morning, I was gloriously baptized with the Holy Spirit. From that day, I began to teach others what I had learned through my experiences. This book gleans from many years of experiences and study of this subject. When we know the promises of God, we cannot be denied. God is a God of promises. He is not a man that He should lie. Everything He promised shall come to pass. As we explore the subject of the Holy Spirit, let us stand on the promises of God, and they shall come to pass just as He said.

# CHAPTER 3

# THE 31 BENEFITS
# OF THE HOLY SPIRIT

Everything about the Holy Spirit is what moves us from operating from the natural to the supernatural. When the Holy Spirit comes, he adds the Super to the natural. He accelerates the natural until it changes into the supernatural. It is like when we heat ice cubes. The molecules of the solid ice begin to expand triggering the ice cube to break up. The more we keep heating it, the molecules expand even faster, and they suddenly turn into liquid water. If we keep on applying the heat, those molecules will become even more accelerated into becoming vapor and will quickly vanish into the air. That process describes the work of the Holy Spirit in a nutshell. He takes us as we are and turns our lives around until we grow from being a natural man to a supernatural man. Think about it. One minute you walk into a room and find a pile of solid ice. The next thing you know, all the ice has melted and turned into an invisible gas. Though unseen, the ice still exists but in a different form.

1.　The Holy Spirit brings power/dunamis. This power helps us to minister and live a victorious life.

"But you shall receive power (ability, efficiency, and might) when the Holy Spirit has come upon you, and you shall be My witnesses in Jerusalem and all Judea and Samaria and to the ends (the very bounds) of the earth' (Acts 1:8).

2.　He is a helper.

'And I will ask the Father, and He will give you another Comforter (Counselor, Helper, Intercessor, Advocate, Strengthener, and Standby), that He may remain with you forever' (John 14:16).

3.　He is the Spirit of truth. He reveals the truth.

'The Spirit of Truth, Whom the world cannot receive (welcome, take to its heart) because it does not see Him or know and recognize Him. But you know and recognize Him, for He lives with you [constantly] and will be in you' (John 14:17).

4.　He abides and dwells in us.

'And I will ask the Father, and He will give you another Comforter (Counselor, Helper, Intercessor, Advocate,

Strengthener, and Standby), that He may remain with you forever' (John 14:16).

"The Spirit of Truth, Whom the world cannot receive (welcome, take to its heart) because it does not see Him or know and recognize Him. But you know and recognize Him, for He lives with you [constantly] and will be in you' (John 14:17).

'Jesus answered, If a person [really] loves Me, he will keep My word [obey My teaching]; and My Father will love him, and We will come to him and make Our home (abode, special dwelling place) with him' (John 14:23)

5. He is a mighty comforter. He comes alongside to help us.

'And I will ask the Father, and He will give you another Comforter (Counselor, Helper, Intercessor, Advocate, Strengthener, and Standby), that He may remain with you forever' (John 14:16).

6. He convicts the world of sin, righteousness, and judgment. Our work is to preach, but the work of the Holy Spirit is to bring conviction to turn people from sin to righteousness. As believers when we fall short in our walk with God, the Holy Spirit convicts us to repent.

'And when He comes, He will convict and convince the world and bring demonstration to it about sin and about righteousness (uprightness of heart and right standing with God) and about judgment' (John 16:8).

7.     He is a guide. He guides us into all truth. When He leads, and we follow, we shall never be in deception again. We shall have the ability to discern the truth.

'But when He, the Spirit of Truth (the Truth-giving Spirit) comes, He will guide you into all the Truth (the whole, full Truth). For He will not speak His own message [on His own authority]; but He will tell whatever He hears [from the Father; He will give the message that has been given to Him], and He will announce and declare to you the things that are to come [that will happen in the future]' (John 16:13).

8.     He reveals what is in the mind of God. Whatever He hears He will speak, and He will tell us things to come. The Holy Spirit knows your future. He is willing to reveal it to you!

'But when He, the Spirit of Truth (the Truth-giving Spirit) comes, He will guide you into all the Truth (the whole, full Truth). For He will not speak His own message [on His own authority]; but He will tell whatever He hears [from the Father; He will give the message that has been given to Him], and He will announce and declare to you the things that are to come [that will happen in the future]' (John 16:13).

## 9.    He glorifies Jesus.

'He will honor and glorify Me, because He will take off
(receive, draw upon) what is Mine and will reveal (declare, disclose, transmit) it to you' (John 16:14).

## 10.    He brings the anointing. Whenever the Holy Spirit comes, the anointing increases.

'How God anointed and consecrated Jesus of Nazareth
with the [Holy] Spirit and with strength and ability and
power; how He went about doing good and, [a]in
particular, curing all who were harassed and oppressed
by [the power of] the devil, for God was with Him' (Acts
10:38).

After being filled with the Holy Spirit, Jesus stated:

The Spirit of the Lord [is] upon Me, because He has
anointed Me [the Anointed One, the Messiah] to preach
the good news (the Gospel) to the poor; He has sent Me
to announce release to the captives and recovery of sight
to the blind, to send forth as delivered those who are
oppressed [who are downtrodden, bruised, crushed, and
broken down by calamity]' (Luke 4:18).

If we knew how to use the power of the Holy Spirit, we
would become very sensitive and depend completely on Him
and not on other resources. That is what Zechariah realized
when he said:

'Then he said to me, this [addition of the bowl to the candlestick, causing it to yield a ceaseless supply of oil from the olive trees] is the word of the Lord to Zerubbabel, saying, Not by might, nor by power, but by My Spirit [of Whom the oil is a symbol], says the Lord of hosts' (Zechariah 4:6).

11.  He helps us with prayer and intercession. He prays a perfect prayer that is exactly in the will of God one hundred percent of all times! The Holy Spirit uses our tongue to make intercession and to pray according to the will of God.

'So too the [Holy] Spirit comes to our aid and bears us up in our weakness; for we do not know what prayer to offer nor how to offer it worthily as we ought, but the Spirit Himself goes to meet our supplication and pleads in our behalf with unspeakable yearning and groaning too deep for utterance. And He Who searches the hearts of men knows what is in the mind of the [Holy] Spirit [what His intent is] because the Spirit intercedes and pleads [before God] in behalf of the saints according to and in harmony with God's will' (Romans 8:26-27).

12.  The Holy Spirit raised Jesus from the dead. He is the resurrection power of God.

'And if the Spirit of Him Who raised up Jesus from the dead dwells in you, [then] He Who raised up Christ Jesus from the dead will also restore to life your mortal (short-lived, perishable) bodies through His Spirit Who dwells in you' (Romans 8:11).

He gives life to our mortal bodies. Strength – physical, spiritual, emotional - strength can come through the Holy Spirit. 'And if the Spirit of Him Who raised up Jesus from the dead dwells in you, [then] He Who raised up Christ Jesus from the dead will also restore to life your mortal (short-lived, perishable) bodies through His Spirit Who dwells in you' (Romans 8:11).

13.　He leads.

'For all who are led by the Spirit of God are sons of God' (Romans 8:14).

14.　He is the Spirit of adoption to help us understand sonship and receive our inheritance in Christ.

'For [the Spirit which] you have now received [is] not a spirit of slavery to put you once more in bondage to fear, but you have received the Spirit of adoption [the Spirit producing sonship] in [the bliss of] which we cry, Abba (Father)! Father! The Spirit Himself [thus] testifies together with our own spirit, [assuring us] that we are children of God. 17And if we are [His] children, then we are [His] heirs also: heirs of God and fellow heirs with Christ [sharing His inheritance with Him]; only we must share His suffering if we are to share His glory' (Romans 8:15-17).

15. He gives us total liberty. The Holy Spirit gives us freedom in the spirit. It is an inside-out experience of being free of every mindset and constraint. Deliverance is not complete until the Holy Spirit comes in to occupy the space that was previously inhabited by other influences. That is why where the Holy Spirit is in full control, there is true freedom. For the Holy Spirit to have full control, he needs to be given full liberty. This comes by yielding ourselves to him.

'Now the Lord is the Spirit, and where the Spirit of the Lord is, there is liberty (emancipation from bondage, freedom)' 'Now the Lord is the Spirit, and where the Spirit of the Lord is, there is liberty (emancipation from bondage, freedom)' (2 Cor 3:17).

16. He is a transforming spirit. The Holy Spirit is not just a great comforter but also a great transformer. He takes us from glory to glory. That is from a lower level of God's intimacy and presence to a higher dimension of glory. There is no end to this transformation. That is why when the Spirit of the Lord comes upon us and continues to fill us, we will never be the same again. When Isaiah experienced the Holy Spirit, he cried, "Woe to me I am ruined; I am undone; I am doomed." This is a cry of a man who knew he would never be the same again. This

level of transformation is irreversible and irrevocable. I pray we begin to experience this dimension of transformation. (2Cor 3:18).

17. He brings the fruit of the spirit. His presence in us begins to bear fruit.

'But the fruit of the [Holy] Spirit [the work which His presence within accomplishes] is love, joy (gladness), peace, patience (an even temper, forbearance), kindness, goodness (benevolence), faithfulness, Gentleness (meekness, humility), self-control (self-restraint, continence). Against such things, there is no law [that can bring a charge]' (Gal 5:22-23).

Fruit is the various aspects that bear evidence of who the Holy Spirit is. Fruit grows. It also gets mature and sweeter. The fruit of the Holy Spirit in us must continue to grow and mature in sweetness and more fruitfulness. Never stop growing in the fruit of the Spirit.

18. He brings the gifts of the spirit into our lives.

'Now there are distinctive varieties and distributions of endowments (gifts, extraordinary powers distinguishing certain Christians, due to the power of divine grace operating in their souls by the Holy Spirit) and they vary, but the [Holy] Spirit remains the same. And there are distinctive varieties of service and ministration, but it is the same Lord [Who is served]. And there are distinctive varieties of operation [of working to accomplish things], but it is the same God Who inspires and energizes them all in all. But to each one is given the manifestation of the [Holy] Spirit [the evidence, the spiritual illumination of the Spirit] for good and profit. To one is given in and through the [Holy] Spirit [the power to speak] a message of wisdom, and to another [the power to express] a word of knowledge and understanding according to the same [Holy] Spirit; To another [wonder-working] faith by the same [Holy] Spirit, to another the extraordinary powers of healing by the one Spirit; To another the working of miracles, to another prophetic insight ([c]the gift of interpreting the divine will and purpose); to another the ability to discern and distinguish between [the utterances of true] spirits [and false ones], to another various kinds of [unknown] tongues, to another the ability to interpret [such] tongues. 11All these [gifts, achievements, abilities] are inspired and brought to pass by one and the same [Holy] Spirit, Who apportions to each person individually [exactly] as He chooses' (1Cor 12:4-11).

These gifts belong to the Holy Spirit. That is why they are called the gifts of the Spirit. They not only represent what the Holy Spirit has but also who He is. He is the Spirit of healing, miracles, faith, wisdom, knowledge, discernment, tongues, tongues interpretation and prophecy. Every aspect of the gifts is a reflection of the nature of God manifested. The Holy Spirit wants to bring out the image and likeness of

God in and through us. He wants to allow the nature of God to grow through us even as the gifts of the Holy Spirit begin to manifest. Desire those gifts. Lust for them. Hunger for them. Eagerly and earnestly covet them. Always understand, there is no limit to the depth, width, height and breadth of how far we can go with the Holy Spirit. His ways are beyond searching. He will take us as far as our hunger will allow. Do not set limits on how far you can desire Him. He will fill you up no matter how deep your longing is.

19. He helps us to overcome the flesh. The Holy Spirit will never allow your flesh to dominate you. The answer for a life dominated by fleshly desires is to receive more of the Holy Spirit.

'But the fruit of the [Holy] Spirit [the work which His presence within accomplishes] is love, joy (gladness), peace, patience (an even temper, forbearance), kindness, goodness (benevolence), faithfulness, Gentleness (meekness, humility), self-control (self-restraint, continence). Against such things, there is no law [that can bring a charge]' (Gal 5:16).

'If we live by the [Holy] Spirit, let us also walk by the Spirit. [If by the Holy Spirit we have our life in God, let us go forward [walking in line, our conduct controlled by the Spirit.]' (Gal 5:25).

20. He brings boldness. When the Holy Spirit comes on us, we become as bold as a lion. Every fear in us

lifts. I have learned to overcome intimidation and fear by boldly embracing the presence of the Holy Spirit.

'And when they had prayed, the place in which they were assembled was shaken; and they were all filled with the Holy Spirit, and they continued to speak the Word of God with freedom and boldness and courage' (Acts 4:31).

21. He turns us into another man. He takes over and makes us someone else other than who we were. He is a different spirit that makes us a different person. What an experience! I have seen this happen in my life. There are times I'm turned into a different man while ministering. I can tell when the transition happens. I can feel the boldness, the anointing, the words and power flowing through me is not my "normal self." It is like being possessed by the Holy Spirit to a level of becoming Holy Spirit possessed- a vessel in his hands.

'Then the Spirit of the Lord will come upon you mightily, and you will show yourself to be a prophet with them; and you will be turned into another man' (1Sam 10:6).

Saul was no longer the same. The Holy Spirit turned him into someone else. Under the anointing of the Holy Spirit, we are no longer the same person. That is why we should handle each other very carefully. We are told to know each other by the Spirit. While a person is speaking or operating under the anointing, we should overcome all our familiarity and respect the office and the anointing under which they are. That way, we are able to tap the benefits of what they bring under the anointing.

22. Through praying in the Holy Spirit, we can build ourselves in pure unadulterated faith. The Holy Spirit edifies a believer and builds up their faith block by block.

'But you, beloved, build yourselves up [founded] on your most holy faith [make progress, rise like an edifice higher and higher], praying in the Holy Spirit;' (Jude 20).

A person is as strong as how much edified they are in the Spirit. It is very clear that when we learn how to pray in the Spirit without ceasing, we are able to build ourselves into a strong house of pure faith. God desires that we build Him a habitation for His glory. If your cry is for the presence of the Lord to abide in you mightily, the best place to start is by building yourself in the holiest faith by praying consistently in the Spirit.

When I pray in tongues, I then wait to hear what God instructs me. Afterward, it is easier to boldly step out in faith to do or speak what the Holy Spirit has revealed. This pure faith is what allows us to be bold and not doubt. The gift of faith operates at its best when we are fully persuaded and fully confident in what we hear from God by the Spirit.

23.  Supernatural strength.

The secret behind the strength of Samson was the Holy Spirit. In various occasions, the Bible would record about the Spirit of the Lord coming upon Samson and moving mightily through him. As a result, he would accomplish mighty deeds. I believe Samson was not a strong man. He was probably a regular average guy with no muscles or stature or any unique natural features. I believe he never looked like anything we see in cartoons and kids bibles or movies. If he looked like that, his strength would be credited to his unique natural characteristics. His victories would not be different from those of Goliath and other giants and mighty men of old. The uniqueness of Samson was that his strength was not by might or power but by the Holy Spirit. The Bible makes this very clear.

In Judges 14:6 the Spirit of the Lord came mightily upon him, and he tore the lion apart like a young goat.

> 'And the Spirit of the Lord came mightily upon him, and he tore the lion as he would have torn a kid, and he had nothing in his hand, but he did not tell his father or mother what he had done.'

In Judges 14:9 the spirit came upon him mightily, and he killed thirty men. '

And he scraped some of the honey out into his hands and went along eating. And he came to his father and mother and gave them some, and they ate it, but he did not tell them he had taken the honey from the body of the lion.'

In Judges 16:9, 11 and14 he broke bonds by the strength of the Holy Spirit. 'Now she had men lying in wait in an inner room. And she said to him, The Philistines are upon you, Samson! And he broke the bowstrings as a string of tow breaks when it touches the fire. So the secret of his strength was not known.'

> 'And he said to her, If they bind me fast with new ropes that have not been used, then I shall become weak and be like any other man.' 'And she did so and fastened it with the pin and said to him, The Philistines are upon you, Samson! And he awoke out of his sleep and went away with the pin of the [weaver's] beam and with the web.'

The strength to kill a thousand men with a jaw bone of a donkey was credited to the power of the Holy Spirit.

> 'And he found a still moist jawbone of a donkey and reached out and took it and slew 1,000 men with it. And Samson said, With the jawbone of a donkey, heaps upon heaps, with the jawbone of a donkey I have slain 1,000 men!' (Judges 15:15-16).

24. The Holy Spirit is described as the seven spirits of the Lord;

"And the Spirit of the Lord shall rest upon Him--the Spirit of wisdom and understanding, the Spirit of counsel and might, the Spirit of knowledge and of the reverential and obedient fear of the Lord—(Isaiah 11:2).

Here we have them all outlined;

    i)    The spirit of the Lord.

    ii)    The spirit of wisdom.

    iii)    The Spirit of understanding.

    iv)    The Spirit of counsel.

    v)    The spirit of might.

    vi)    The Spirit of knowledge

    vii)    The Spirit of the fear of the Lord.

When we receive the Holy Spirit, all the seven spirits of the Lord come with Him. Seven is the number that represents completion. The seven spirits of the Lord represents the fullness of the Spirit dwelling in us.

I love the way Romans 8:11 describes the Holy Spirit as the one that quickens our mortal bodies.

'And if the Spirit of Him Who raised up Jesus from the dead dwells in you, [then] He Who raised up Christ Jesus from the dead will also restore to life your mortal (short-lived, perishable) bodies through His Spirit Who dwells in you.'

It is possible to receive this kind of strength to be able to serve God. This is not mere physical strength. It is spiritual strength manifesting through our physical bodies. With this strength, we can effectively serve God even in dire circumstances. There are times I have been physically drained, but after offering myself as a vessel for God, I end up receiving supernatural strength to be able to minister the word of God. By waiting upon the Lord, He renews our strength, and we can mount up with wings like an eagle. We can run and not grow weary. We can walk and not faint. I thank God for giving me the strength not to cancel any meetings due to sickness or weakness. God's assignment comes with physical strength to accomplish it. Paul learned these secrets many years ago. In 2Cor12:9-10 he found out that the grace of God is sufficient for us [his strength is the supernatural strength of the Holy Spirit] and his strength is made perfect in our weakness.

> 'But He said to me, My grace (My favor and loving-kindness and mercy) is enough for you [sufficient against any danger and enables you to bear the trouble manfully]; for My strength and power are made perfect (fulfilled and completed) and show themselves most effective in [your] weakness. Therefore, I will all the more gladly glory in my weaknesses and infirmities, that the strength and power of Christ (the Messiah) may rest (yes, may pitch a tent over and dwell) upon me, So for the sake of

Christ, I am well pleased and take pleasure in infirmities, insults, hardships, persecutions, perplexities and distresses; for when I am weak [in human strength], then am I [truly] strong (able, powerful in divine strength).'

That's why I am convinced that Samson was not a big man in stature. He was most likely an average man with very limited physical strength. He relied entirely on the strength of the Holy Spirit. That is why He is not described as a giant like Goliath. He was a mere man but under the power of the Holy Spirit. There used to be an 80 years old man of God in the United States. He was one of the greatest missionary evangelists that ever lived. He loved to mentor young people in ministry. Most of those that he worked with are today in the forefront of world evangelism. They say of him that he had so much strength that they could not keep up with him even at such an advanced age!

25.   The ability to take cities for God.

Samson supernaturally under the power of the Holy Spirit took the gates of the city to the top of the hill.

'But Samson lay until midnight, and [then] he arose and took hold of the doors of the city's gate and the two posts, and pulling them up, bar and all, he put them on his shoulders and carried them to the top of the hill that is before Hebron' (Judges 16:3).

This is a prophetic picture of the end time church that would be able to open up cities for God. The gate of the city represents the seat of government power and authority of a territory. God will raise a generation that will take cities by force of the Holy Spirit and break the power of the demonic powers that bind them. In the book of Acts 8:5-8 Philip took an entire city for God by the power of the Holy Spirit.

> 'Philip [the deacon, not the apostle] went down to the city of Samaria and proclaimed the Christ (the Messiah) to them [the people]; And great crowds of people with one accord listened to and heeded what was said by Philip, as they heard him and watched the miracles and wonders which he kept performing [from time to time]. For foul spirits came out of many who were possessed by them, screaming and shouting with a loud voice, and many who were suffering from palsy or were crippled were restored to health. And there was great rejoicing in that city.'

In the last days, the manifestation of the power of the Holy Spirit shall increase within the body of Christ. The Church shall be restored to her authority and power. The gates of hell shall not prevail. Cities will open up for God in such a mighty way. The end time church will be able to bring in the greatest harvest of souls ever witnessed in the earth. They will do it through the power of the Holy Spirit.

26.   He gives the anointing of the overtaker:

This is the ability to be fast-tracked on the fast lane by the supernatural power of the Holy Spirit. Jesus spoke about this anointing of the overtaker in Matt 19:30.

'But many who [now] are first will be last [then], and many who [now] are last will be first [then].'

There shall be a supernatural ability to cause those who are on the bottom of the pile to come on top and those who started late to finish first. Such ability is granted by the Holy Spirit. It is the anointing of the overtaker. Sometimes this anointing manifests as transportations and translations in the spirit. In the Old Testament, Elijah would be transported by the spirit in the natural. After he had declared the famine in Israel for three and a half years, Ahab the king looked for him with an intention to arrest and kill him. The Holy Spirit kept transporting him to different places for his protection.

'As the Lord your God lives, there is no nation or kingdom where my lord has not sent to seek you. And when they said, He is not here, he took an oath from the kingdom or nation that they had not found you. And now you say, Go tell your lord, Behold, Elijah is here. And as soon as I have gone out from you, the Spirit of the Lord will carry you I know not where; so when I come and tell Ahab, and he cannot find you, he will kill me. But I your

servant have feared and revered the Lord from my youth'
(1Kings 18:10-12).

After he had prayed for the rain, the Spirit of God came
upon him, and he was able to overtake Ahab's chariot. Even
the fastest chariots of the time would not be able to out-run
him.

"The hand of the Lord was on Elijah. He girded up his
loins and ran before Ahab to the entrance of Jezreel
[nearly twenty miles]' (1Kings 18:46).

In the New Testament Philip experienced transporta-
tion in the spirit.

'And when they came up out of the water, the Spirit of
the Lord [suddenly] caught away Philip; and the eunuch
saw him no more, and he went on his way rejoicing'
(Acts8:39).

If you look up the distance, it was 90 miles away.

The Holy Spirit can transport us with an accelerated
speed both in the natural and in the spiritual realm. In Amos
9:13 the plower shall overtake the reaper. The treader of
grapes shall overtake the sower of the seed.

'Behold, the days are coming, says the Lord, that the
plowman shall overtake the reaper, and the treader of
grapes him who sows the seed; and the mountains shall
drop sweet wine and all the hills shall melt [that is,

everything heretofore barren and unfruitful shall overflow with spiritual blessing].'

This is a prophetic illustration of a season of incredible overtaking both in the spirit and natural realm. It describes a situation where seasons collapse on each other. Harvest time would come even before the sowing time is done. When the anointing of the overtaker comes upon a person, business, church, or family; it accelerates the speed of blessing and restoration in their lives. This anointing also breaks the power of delay and ushers in a season of extreme restoration and prosperity. The anointing of the over-taker ensures that we are restored to where we should have been by now. It also erases the years that were wasted through delays, distractions, being stuck in a rut, and detours of destiny.

What does this anointing mean to a family who has gone through divorce? It means that the days that were wasted and the momentum that was lost shall be regained. God will supernaturally get you up to speed. That also applies to businesses that have gone through bankruptcy, loss, and destruction. Even churches that have been held back from taking territory and making progress, the anointing of the overtaker is going to be manifested. The word of Jesus Christ will never fall on the ground 'the first shall be last, and the last shall be first.'

We need access to hidden things. God hides things not from us but for us. Several things in the Bible are hidden, and they need a key to access them.

27.    Holy Spirit gives supernatural access by key of David.

The key of David is mentioned twice in the Bible. In Isaiah 22:22 and Revelation 3:7.

This key is placed on the shoulder and whatever door it opens no one can shut and whatever door it shuts no one can open.

> 'And the key of the house of David I will lay upon his shoulder; he shall open, and no one shall shut, he shall shut, and no one shall open.'

Ultimately this is the master key to the kingdom of God. Shoulders stand for the ability to carry governmental responsibilities. It is a supernatural governmental ability to gain access with no restriction whatsoever. It is the highest security clearance that can ever be granted to someone. In earthly governments, senior officials are granted different levels of security clearance. Such a clearance gives them access to files, documents and places of high security and classified information. Without such information, it is impossible for a government leader to make decisions concerning a situation. This level of access is the evidence of the trust that has been bestowed on a person. That is why every door that is opened or closed by the key of David cannot be undone because only that key of David can undo it. This supernatural ability is granted through revelation knowledge by the Holy Spirit. No one can access the key of David except by the Holy Spirit.

## WHY DO WE NEED THE KEY OF DAVID?

We need access to hidden things. God hides things not from us but for us. Several things in the Bible are hidden, and they need a key to access them.

i) Hidden pot of manna which symbolizes hidden revelation knowledge of God's word.

The hidden pot of manna is the food that was given to the children of Israel in the wilderness. This food was supernaturally provided by God from heaven. It was the food of angels who are the mighty servants of God. Manna is food that is released to feed those who want to be mighty in God. It refers to feeding in the revelation of God's word. Hidden manna is not hidden or concealed from us, but to the contrary, it is hidden or set aside and preserved for the ones who seek to find it. It is only available to those who want to go an extra mile in seeking God. The hidden pot of manna is inside the ark of the covenant, inside the holy of holies. Notice the place where this pot was hidden. It was in the innermost chamber of the Tabernacle and locked in the most secure place in the entire tabernacle. For one to access the hidden pot of manna, they had to go through three chambers. This is symbolic of the depth in intimacy and seeking God. This also shows the depth needed in seeking God by the words of Jesus in Matthew 7:7;

   a)   ask and keep on asking level of prayer and intimacy.

   b)   seek and keep on seeking level of prayer and intimacy.

   c)   knock and keep on knocking level of prayer and intimacy.

There is such a depth in pursuing the presence of God releasing the manifestation in the hidden manna that can only be found in the intimate place of worship and walk with God. That is where you get a fresh word from heaven. It comes like fresh manna [ food for the mighty servants of God]. Such a word can turn your life around and give you the strength to finish the journey. Jesus said, 'man shall not live by bread alone but by every word that proceeds out the mouth of God.' Power to live and keep on living through the word that is released afresh from the mouth of God. Access to the pot of hidden manna is granted by the Holy Spirit through the key of worship.

   ii)   Hidden riches of the secret places.

In Isaiah 45:3 the bible clearly states the place of hidden riches of secret places.

> 'And I will give you the treasures of darkness and hidden riches of secret places, that you may know that it is I, the Lord, the God of Israel, Who calls you by your name.'

The word secret place is the same one found in Psalms 91:1.

> 'He who dwells in the secret place of the Most High shall remain stable and fixed under the shadow of the Almighty [Whose power no foe can withstand].'

There is a place called the secret place. The treasures of God are found in the secret place. The hidden riches of the power, presence, and love of God are found in the secret place. [Supernatural wealth in all realms spiritual, material and natural is found in the secret place]. Again as I said earlier, those who know how to access the secret place of the most high God will find the hidden riches found in the secret place. Business leaders, scientists, and ministers of the gospel shall receive instructions and divine revelation stored in the secret place. The secret of being mighty in God and the power to do mighty exploits is found in our intimacy with the Lord in the secret places. The depth of the revelation provides rich spiritual meat to make us strong and mighty to walk in the supernatural power of God.

In Proverbs 8:12 the bible says

> 'I wisdom dwell with prudence, and find out knowledge of witty inventions.'

There is a place in God where He can reveal patterns, models and scientific information that can bring scientific breakthroughs into the natural realm. No wonder most of the scientists and inventors of old were men and women of God. They created their inventions through supernatural revelation. They were able to operate in a spiritual mind which is also the mind of Christ. As a result, they accessed the realm of knowledge that Adam had before the fall. This realm is not accessed through academic accomplishments. Adam did not have a college degree. He had the Spirit of God working in and through him. He was spiritually minded and had access to the mind of Christ. The mind of Christ is an anointed mind where thoughts, intentions, and imaginations are led of the Spirit. If a business man goes before the Lord and accesses hidden riches of secret places, he can come out with business models and strategies that will defy every competition. God wants to restore this kind of knowledge and hidden riches of the secret places. We must be ready to seek his face. This is the time for a mighty restoration in the name of Jesus Christ! The church must walk in her full measure of power. Oh, what a great day we are living in!

iii)   Things hidden from the wise have been revealed to little children.

'In that same hour He rejoiced and gloried in the Holy Spirit and said, I thank You, Father, Lord of heaven and earth, that You have concealed these things [relating to salvation] from the wise and understanding and learned, and revealed them to babes (the childish, unskilled, and untaught). Yes, Father, for such was Your gracious will and choice and good pleasure' (Luke 10:21).

The secrets of the kingdom of God are given to those who are humble and meek. It is those who have a child-like faith. Humility and meekness is not weakness, it is rather a strength under control. The meek will inherit the earth. They shall rule because they are strong. Through the attributes of humility, the strength of the kingdom is manifested. The things of the Spirit are foolishness to the people of the world. They are spiritually discerned.

'But the natural, nonspiritual man does not accept or welcome or admit into his heart the gifts and teachings and revelations of the Spirit of God, for they are folly (meaningless nonsense) to him; and he is incapable of knowing them [of progressively recognizing, understanding, and becoming better acquainted with them] because they are spiritually discerned and estimated and appreciated' (1Cor2:14).

iv) God has also entrusted the things of the kingdom to the foolish.

'[This is] because the foolish thing [that has its source in] God is wiser than men, and the weak thing [that springs] from God is stronger than men. For [simply] consider your own call, brethren; not many [of you were considered to be] wise according to human estimates and standards, not many influential and powerful, not many of high and noble birth. [No] for God selected (deliberately chose) what in the world is foolish to put the wise to shame, and what the world calls weak to put the strong to shame. And God also selected (deliberately chose) what in the world is lowborn and insignificant and branded and treated with contempt, even the things that are nothing, that He might depose and bring to nothing the things that are, So that no mortal man should [have pretense for glorying and] boast in the presence of God' (1Cor 1:25-29).

The kingdom of God is an upside down kingdom. He calls those who are not mighty, not wise or noble. He chooses the foolish things of this world [weak things; base things]. Then He pours His spirit into such vessels to gain glory that no flesh should glory in His presence.

The attitude of humility and childlike faith is the key to accessing the hidden things of the kingdom. The lower you go in humility, the higher you rise in being exalted by God.

v)     Treasure hidden in a field.

'The kingdom of heaven is like something precious buried in a field, which a man found and hid again; then in his joy, he goes and sells all he has and buys that field' (Matt 13:44).

Those who find the wealth concealed in the principles of the kingdom of God will in return access everything else. Jesus also said that if we seek first the kingdom of God and all righteousness, EVERYTHING ELSE (including all that we would ever desire or want to be) shall be added to us (Matthew 6:33). The wealth of the Kingdom of God is beyond estimation. Just the wisdom of God alone is worth more than silver, gold, and rubies. Abundant life [spirit, soul, and body] is found in the Kingdom of God. Untold wealth, riches, and honor are in the house of the Lord. The Kingdom of God is not just about us getting saved and going to heaven. Satan knows the wealth of the Kingdom of God. He used to enjoy the best of Gods' kingdom. He used to dwell in the presence of God as a worship leader. God had given him supernatural glory and splendor. He was clothed with every kind of instrument for making music and melodies. He was covered in glory and precious jewels. That is why he uses temptations against God's people. A temptation would not be truly a temptation unless it is trying to take something more valuable in exchange for a counterfeit. What Satan has to offer is of a lower quality than what God has given to us. When the Holy Spirit opens our eyes through wisdom and revelation, we are able to see the hidden treasures of the Kingdom of God. Such a revelation will cause a person to abandon everything in pursuit of the Kingdom of God. Anything we need or ever want to be is hidden for us in the Kingdom of God. When we lay something down for the Kingdom of God, it does not leave our lives. It comes back to us redeemed and sanctified for His glory.

Jesus knew that we need things in our lives. Some of them are spiritual, material, emotional, or relational. He assured us that they are all made available through the Kingdom of God. In Christ, all treasures, all wisdom, all knowledge, all riches, all grace, all truth, all blessings, greatness, promises, revelation, joy, and everlasting peace is found in Him.

> "For it was in Him that all things were created, in heaven and on earth, things seen and things unseen, whether thrones, dominions, rulers, or authorities; all things were created and exist through Him [by His service, intervention] and in and for Him. 'And He Himself existed before all things, and in Him, all things consist (cohere, are held together)' (Col 1:16-17).

In Him, all things exist. He is all in all. Whoever finds him finds everything.

28.   Supernatural wisdom and revelation.

The Holy Spirit grants us supernatural wisdom and revelation in both natural and supernatural matters. To be spiritually minded is to have the ability to operate in the mind of Christ. A spiritually minded person has wisdom beyond their years. They possess knowledge beyond their academic qualifications. Their source of information, reasoning, and application of knowledge is the Holy Spirit. Adam displayed the power of a spiritually minded person. He had no books, no schooling, no parental guidance, no mentorship, or any natural means of learning. In spite of all those limitations, Adam was able to manage the whole creation and also name all the animals in the garden. Joseph and Daniel were top government advisors. They were credited for having supernatural wisdom. Pharaoh, the king of Egypt, handed over the reigns of power to Joseph because of his wisdom. Pharaoh recognized that Joseph's wisdom was from the Lord. It had nothing to do with his schooling or philosophical power. Daniel served eight heathen kings as a high-ranking advisor. He was in high demand in eight regimes because of his spiritual wisdom. If we operate in the wisdom of God through the Holy Spirit, even the worldly government systems will take notice. Paul prayed for the church of Ephesus to receive the spirit of wisdom and revelation in the knowledge of God.

> "[For I always pray to] the God of our Lord Jesus Christ, the Father of glory, that He may grant you a spirit of wisdom and revelation [of insight into mysteries and secrets] in the [deep and intimate] knowledge of Him" (Eph 1:17).

Notice this prayer is not for wisdom and revelation. Paul specifically asked for the Spirit of wisdom and the Spirit of revelation. Paul asked for a continuous streaming of the Spirit of God to bring wisdom and revelation as needed in a ceaseless manner. That's exactly what we need today. We need all the branches of wisdom for any area of life. This wisdom will grant us mastery in family, relationships, finances, business, science, inventions, government, cultural trends, fashion, music, literature, arts and all areas of life. It will come as understanding, revelation, knowledge, prudence, discernment and discretion.

29. He gives a believer an added advantage in any situation.

We live in two worlds. We have the natural and the spiritual world. We have more than just the natural tools. We have access to a huge deposit of spiritual tools at our disposal. We should learn how to activate the spiritual dimension in any given situation. We can look at things from spiritual and natural perspectives. We can also hear from the natural and spiritual dimension. This advantage to operate in two realms is only available to the believer. The realm of the spirit is superior to the natural realm. When something is blocked in the natural, we can unblock it from the spirit. When there is confusion in the natural can fight it from the spiritual. The ability to influence the spirit realm is restricted only to those who are familiar with its inner-workings. Jesus said that it is to our advantage that He goes to heaven because that is the only way that the Holy Spirit will come. That is what "the Holy Ghost Advantage" is all about. Some people like to say that the Holy Ghost is the Ghost with the most! Think about it. A Holy Ghost filled businessman has more tools to make strategic plans than those who don't have the power of the Holy Ghost.

When I function as a consultant, I have seen how awesome it is to access the prophetic gifts. I counsel global leaders and business people. I speak into the lives of decision makers on matters of leadership development and capacity building. There are times I have been in boardrooms or business meetings. Other times in my practice I have had to pray about what to tell my clients. Through the Holy Spirit, I am able to hear the voice of the Lord and give them a word that ends up being the key to their breakthrough. One time I was about to make a presentation in front of some national leaders of a foreign government. I knew that this was the time to access the favor of the king. I spent a lot of time in prayer. During my time in the waiting room, I continued praying in tongues under my breath. When it came to the time of making the presentation, I cannot tell you how eloquent and polished I sounded. But one thing I can tell you is that the outcome of the entire experience was nothing but epic. What could not happen through my limited knowledge in diplomacy and public relations was able to happen by the Holy Spirit. He is indeed the Ghost with the most.

30.  Supernatural protection.

Psalms 105 says, 'touch not my anointed and do my prophets no harm.' The anointing of the Holy Spirit is a covering that protects the person and the office on which the anointing rests. The anointing of the Holy Spirit destroys the yokes and removes the burdens. Also, where the anointing of God is resident, there is special deployment of angels. These angels protect the glory of God from being defiled. That is why it is impossible for anything to mess up with what God has anointed. David understood that when Samuel poured oil on Saul, regardless of his character, the anointing protected him. David refrained from killing Saul or his family. He left everything in the hands of God. Psalms 91 outlines the full package benefits of hiding in the secret place (which is the covering of the anointing) of the most high. These benefits cover provision, protection, and long life. I have learned that the best thing to do is to get people under the anointing of the Holy Spirit and let him do the rest. Ultimately, he knows what's best for us.

The best place to hide is under the anointing of the Holy Spirit. The anointing itself removes the burdens and destroys the yokes. Anything that tries to tamper with us is considered a burden or a yoke. In such a situation, the anointing will fight for us. I have no fear as long as I am anointed. I know that the anointing will protect me and avenge/vindicate for me. That is why it is important we know how to handle each other. Many people have died early or fallen into sicknesses and weaknesses for mishandling the body of Christ. We should do everything to respect the anointing on each other's lives and treat it with honor. We must master relationships, overcome familiarity by respecting the office and the anointing on people's lives. Always remember, there are special blessing and reward for receiving a prophet in the name of the prophet. God said to Abraham that He would bless those who bless him and curse those who curse him (Gen 12: 1-2)

Jesus reminded us that if we receive a prophet in the name of a prophet we shall receive a prophet's reward. The way we receive a prophet determines what kind of rewards we receive. Prophetic anointing carries prophetic rewards. Those rewards are like a packaged deal that is accessed through the way you receive the prophet. It is possible to receive a prophet correctly or wrongly. It is your choice. You can eat with a prophet, be married to a prophet, sleep with a prophet and never receive anything from his anointing or mantle just because of the way you handle the prophet. Those who receive the prophet rightly will profit. Sometimes there are things that will be cut off from your life because you have been faithful in receiving people that God has anointed and prepared for this generation. In the Bible, Dorcas was raised from the dead by how she operated in the gift and grace of hospitality. Death was suspended from her life, and she was raised up to live a full life to fulfill her destiny. You too will be protected from death and destruction because of your faithfulness in handling the anointing.

31.   The Holy Spirit is one of the chief agents in the creation of anything new. When God speaks something, the Holy Spirit responds by bringing it into manifestation. He creates, he forms and he reforms.

I will outline the ten major examples of the Holy Spirit at the creating and inception of things:

i)   IN THE BEGINNING: Gen 1:2, in the beginning, the Holy Spirit moved over the face of the waters.

'The earth was without form and an empty waste, and darkness was upon the face of the very great deep. The Spirit of God was moving (hovering, brooding) over the face of the waters.'

When God began to speak, everything He said, the Holy Spirit performed. Whenever God initiates something, it is the Holy Spirit that performs and perfects it. He is still perfecting the church that He birthed. His work in our lives is to perfect all that concerns us.

ii)   IN THE CREATION OF MAN: During the creation of man, God consulted with Jesus and the Holy Spirit. This again proves that God will never do anything without involving the Holy Spirit. The Holy Spirit is a very key player in the initiation of new things.

'God said, Let Us [Father, Son, and Holy Spirit] make mankind in Our image, after Our likeness, and let them have complete authority over the fish of the sea, the birds of the air, the [tame] beasts, and over all of the earth, and over everything that creeps upon the earth.' (Gen 1:26).

iii)   **BREATHING LIFE INTO MAN:** After creating man, God the Father breathed His spirit into the lifeless body of Adam. Before Adam could possess life, it was the Holy Spirit that was involved in quickening his mortal body. He made it possible for Adam to function as a human being. The Holy Spirit gave him the unction to function.

What Adam received was what we call in Greek, Pneuma. It is the life-giving Spirit of God. It is also what made Adam a speaking spirit complete with the image and likeness of God. Indeed, the fullness of the image and likeness of God is produced when we receive the fullness of the Holy Spirit.

iv)   **IN BIRTHING OF THE NATION OF ISRAEL:** During the birth of the nation of Israel on Mount Sinai, the Holy Spirit was also involved. The timing was on the day of the Feast of Pentecost. Just like in the upper room, the Holy Spirit came as wind, fire and an earthquake that shook the mountain. Moses' face began to shine in glory. The nation of Israel was mid-wifed by the Holy Spirit.

v) **IN INAUGURATION OF KINGS, PROPHETS, PRIESTS AND JUDGES OF ISRAEL:** The birthing of kings, prophets, and judges in the nation of Israel was also by the Holy Spirit. Nobody became a king in Israel without first being anointed with the horn of oil that symbolized the outpouring of the Holy Spirit on them. This outpouring was the first thing that happened to put someone on the legitimate office in the nation of Israel. In the life of David, he was anointed three times. Each anointing marked a new expansion of his authority and realm of rule. The Holy Spirit was not only involved in installing David on the throne but also in birthing the expansion of each level of his realm of rule. David operated as a king, a judge, a prophet, and a priest.

vi) **WHEN RECEIVING NEW IDEAS:** The entry of wisdom creates new ideas and concepts given by the Holy Spirit. No new idea, discovery, concept, invention, or even a song is released into the realm of the natural except by the spirit. The Holy Spirit is the source of all God-things being released into the earthly realm. He is the Spirit of wisdom and revelation.

vii) **THE CONCEPTION OF JESUS:** Jesus was conceived in the womb of Mary by the Holy Spirit.

The Angel of the Lord promised that the Holy Spirit would overshadow her and that which will be born will be called the Son of God.

'Then the angel said to her, The Holy Spirit will come upon you, and the power of the Most High will overshadow you [like a shining cloud]; and so the holy (pure, sinless) Thing (Offspring) which shall be born of you will be called the Son of God' (Luke 1:35).

Even Jesus could not be born except by the Holy Spirit. God wants to overshadow us by the Holy Spirit. He will bring to pass the birthing of awesome things in our lives. Each one of them will have a name. This book was birthed through the overshadowing of the Holy Spirit. In 1993, I became pregnant with a ministry of destiny after being overshadowed by the Holy Spirit. This is the time to be overshadowed by the Holy Spirit and also birth things that are going to eternally change the landscape of the world around us. It could be new businesses, new inventions, new churches, new ministries, new songs or new revolutionary ideas.

viii) DURING THE RESURRECTION OF JESUS: It was the Holy Spirit who raised Jesus from the dead.

'And if the Spirit of Him Who raised up Jesus from the dead dwells in you, [then] He Who raised up Christ Jesus from the dead will also restore to life your mortal (short-lived, perishable) bodies through His Spirit Who dwells in you'(Romans 8:11).

He made the spirit of Jesus to be reunited with His body which caused the resurrection to take place. This made Jesus become the first fruits of creation. When the Holy Spirit comes, He gives new life to dead things. He causes them to have a new beginning. Many of us have gone through seasons of death and destruction. Sometimes it feels like we are totally finished. God wants to cause a new life to begin. It will take the Holy Spirit to bring into being a new life. Do you need a resurrection? Are you coming from a season of experiences that nearly annihilated your life? Maybe you faced a devastating divorce, a bankruptcy, a loss of a job, a broken relationship, a near-death experience or a shattered dream. The Holy Spirit breathes life into the broken pieces of your past to give you a new beginning. He is the same Spirit that raised Jesus from the dead. Let Him raise you up too.

ix) DURING THE BIRTH OF THE EARLY CHURCH AS WE KNOW IT: The Holy Spirit birthed the Church in the upper room on the day of the feast of Pentecost. Just like He birthed the nation of Israel on the day of the Feast of Pentecost, so did He birth the church in Acts 2:1-4. He came in with fire as a mighty rushing wind that shook the building. He birthed the church as a mighty force just like the nation of Israel. It is the greatest institution that has ever been created in the history of the world. There has never been anything like the church, and there will never be. The church was born by the Holy Spirit to be filled with the Holy Spirit, sustained by the Holy Spirit, lead by the Holy Spirit, perfected by the Holy Spirit, and presented to Jesus by the Holy Spirit. If we can give the church back to the Holy Spirit, He will restore her into a mighty army, purified without spot or wrinkle.

x)  DURING OUR NEW BIRTH EXPERIENCE: The Holy Spirit is the primary agent involved in our new birth experience. Nobody can be born again except by the Holy Spirit. Nobody can even say that Jesus is Lord except by the Holy Spirit. The conviction to salvation is the primary ministry of the Holy Spirit. Conviction happens before anybody can come to Christ. The Holy Spirit makes us a new creation. He takes away the old and makes all things new.

These ten examples can lay out the case that everything begins by the Spirit and ends by the Spirit. If the Holy Spirit is the author, He should also be the finisher. It is very critical to never do away with the Holy Spirit. The same way the Spirit brings things into being, He also reveals and takes them to the next level. The Holy Spirit is for today. If you let Him lead you, He will take you places you have never imagined.

# CHAPTER 4.

# HOW TO BE FILLED WITH THE HOLY SPIRIT

The Holy Spirit comes into our lives by invitation. We must show a desire for the Holy Spirit and then ask Him to come in. He is the source of our supply, and we are His vessels. That relationship must be kept in perspective by those who are receiving the Holy Spirit. The vessel must be empty. It must also be positioned under the Holy Spirit so that the oil can flow in. This is a relationship of being submitted and subject to the Holy Spirit. The vessel must also be fully yielded and set apart only for the master. He does not mix Himself with another. The Holy Spirit will not be a part of other spirits. He is either the Lord of all or not the Lord at all. We serve a jealous God. He is a jealous lover. He refuses to be an amalgamation of other things. He is not one of the ways. He is the ONLY way. He is not one

of the gods. He is the only God. His kingdom does not negotiate with other kingdoms. He takes over other kingdoms and enlarges His rule and reign. He dethrones all the previous masters and regimes so that He can rule and reign in their stead. When we understand that spiritual protocol, we can rightfully welcome and host the Holy Spirit.

Paul spoke of this relationship in 2 Tim 2:20-21.

'In a large house there are articles not only of gold and silver but also of wood and clay; some are for special purposes and some for common use. Those who cleanse themselves from the latter will be instruments for special purposes, made holy, useful to the Master and prepared to do any good work.'

He challenged believers to make themselves available as a vessel of honor, sanctified and useful for the Master. The Holy Spirit requires a believer to hunger for Him. Whatever we do to create an atmosphere of hunger, passion, and desperation for Him, it will create room for the flow of the Holy Spirit into a vessel. The Bible gives several illustrations of how we can be filled with Holy Spirit.

1.   By persistent prayer

Jesus spoke to the disciples to be persistent in their prayer.

"Ask and it will be given to you; seek and you will find; knock and the door will be opened to you. For everyone who asks receives; the one who seeks finds; and to the one who knocks, the door will be opened. 'Which of you, if your son asks for bread, will give him a stone? Or if he asks for a fish, will give him a snake? If you, then, though you are evil, know how to give good gifts to your children, how much more will your Father in heaven give good gifts to those who ask him!" (Matthew 7:7-11).

In the Luke Gospel He says,

"Which of you fathers, if your son asks for a fish, will give him a snake instead? Or if he asks for an egg, will give him a scorpion? If you then, though you are evil, know how to give good gifts to your children, how much more will your Father in heaven give the Holy Spirit to those who ask him!" (Luke 11:11-13).

He gave three levels of persistence:

i)   Asking-When we know the will of God as revealed by His Word, we have a blood-bought right to ask for it in prayer. Never stop asking God to fill you. That constant state of pursuit is a sign of a desperate hunger that cannot be denied. We must become persistent and refuse to be refused. We must deny being denied. We must never let go until we receive. There's that "until factor." It is an attitude that knows that we know that we know what we know that we know that we know that God has promised it and He will perform it!

ii) Seeking- Sometimes we need to go to the next gear of asking. This is what I call seeking. Seek His face with all your heart, soul and mind. It may take a lot of praying, diligent study of God's word, waiting and even fasting. Do whatever it takes. Seek His will, seek His truth, seek His desire and make it yours. Never give up in seeking. Only those who seek will find. Seeking does not mean that God is hiding. It is not like a game of hide and seek. God loves it when we tag on Him by being in a diligent pursuit through seeking Him.

iii) Knocking at the door- This is the next gear up in our seeking. When we want to take our seeking prayers to the next level, we begin to knock on the door. It is like some barren women I have prayed for. Some have gone home and bought diapers, prepared baby rooms and started getting ready for the baby. They constantly enter into the baby room to remind God that their persistence in prayer has gone to the next level. They line up their faith with actions. Stay at the door and keep on knocking because there is nowhere else to go but to the Lord. He will open the door. The law of demand and supply in the spirit guarantees that as long as we put a demand on Him, He will supply. Sometimes it takes an intense upping of our pursuit. God loves it when we tag on Him like a father whose sons tag on Him. This level of prayer cannot be denied.

I prophesy to you in the name of Jesus that you are at the door of your miracle. If you knock and keep on knocking without giving up, you shall not be denied. Never give up. You are too close to quit!

Persistent prayer must be specific. It must also increase in intensity. Jesus concluded by saying that if us being evil know how to give good gifts to our children, how much more will our Father in heaven give the Holy Spirit to those who ask? This statement has a lot in common with Matthew 5:6

"Blessed are those who hunger and thirst for righteousness for they shall be filled."

The greater the hunger, the stronger the persistence. When we understand the benefits of the Holy Spirit, we will hunger more for Him. Hunger must be filled before any satisfaction happens. One of the biggest responsibilities of our government is to ensure that their people have food. When a nation goes into hunger, it goes into riots. The lack of hunger in the body of Christ is the root cause of the spiritual lukewarmness that has caused many to be complacent and spiritually dead. In 2Cor 12:31 Paul says, "But earnestly desire the best gifts." The other meaning for the words 'earnest desire' is lusting or craving. This, of course, implies an intense hunger that must be fulfilled. This is love with a passion that is as strong as death. The Holy Spirit must become such a need for us that we cannot live one moment longer without Him.

2.    The laying on of hands

The Holy Spirit can be received by the laying on of hands. Several people in the Bible were filled with the Holy Spirit when spirit filled believers laid hands on them and prayed. In Acts 8:14-17 Peter and John laid hands on the Samaritan believers, and they received the Holy Spirit.

> 'When the apostles in Jerusalem heard that Samaria had accepted the word of God, they sent Peter and John to Samaria. When they arrived, they prayed for the new believers there that they might receive the Holy Spirit because the Holy Spirit had not yet come on any of them; they had simply been baptized in the name of the Lord Jesus. Then Peter and John placed their hands on them, and they received the Holy Spirit.'

In Acts 19:2-6 Paul laid hands on the believers in Ephesus.

> 'and asked them, "Did you receive the Holy Spirit when you believed?"

They answered, "No, we have not even heard that there is a Holy Spirit." So Paul asked, "Then what baptism did you receive?" "John's baptism," they replied. Paul said, "John's baptism was a baptism of repentance. He told the people to believe in the one coming after him, that is, in Jesus." On hearing this, they were baptized in the name of the Lord Jesus. When Paul placed his hands on them, the Holy Spirit came on them, and they spoke in tongues and prophesied.'

The Holy Spirit came upon them, and they spoke with tongues and prophesied. There is power in the laying on of hands. I first received the baptism with the Holy Spirit through the laying on of hands.

The gifts of Holy Spirit can be imparted by the laying on of hands. Also, the baptism of the Holy Spirit can be administered in the same way. Spirit-filled believers have the power to lead others in baptism through the laying on of hands. This practice is a biblical way of acting as a conduit and a point of contact for the transmission of the power of God. One of the most effective ways of administering the Holy Spirit by laying on of hands is to first teach the word and then release the power. Training, teaching and then activation must go hand in hand. When God's word is explained and taught clearly, the heart is prepared for the practical release of that truth by the laying on of hands.

Paul ministered to Timothy on several occasions by teaching and the laying on of hands. He reminded Timothy of the impartation that took place when hands were laid on him. Even in the Old Testament in the book of Deut 34:9 Joshua had the wisdom of the lord because Moses had laid hands on him.

'Now Joshua son of Nun was filled with the spirit of wisdom because Moses had laid his hands on him. So the Israelites listened to him and did what the LORD had commanded Moses.'

### 3.    The breath of the Holy Spirit

In the book of John 20:21-22 Jesus breathed on them, and He said receive the Holy Spirit.

'Then Jesus said to them again, Peace to you! [Just] as the Father has sent Me forth, so I am sending you. And having said this, He breathed on them and said to them, Receive the Holy Spirit!'

This is the same way God breathed into Adam with the breath of life that made him a living being in Genesis 2:7.

'Then the Lord God formed man from the dust of the ground and breathed into his nostrils the breath or spirit of life, and man became a living being.'

The Holy Spirit is the breath of God. The Greek word is pneuma. It is this breath of God that gives life to our spirit man. Breathing the Holy Spirit is a practice that Jesus used in releasing the Holy Spirit to His disciples. That is how He did it in John 20

"'Peace to you! As the Father sent me, I also send you.' And when He had said this, He breathed on them and said, 'Receive the Holy Spirit'" (John 20:21-22, NKJV).

One of the symbols of the Holy Spirit is breath or wind. Without breath, in the natural, a man is considered dead. This means that the Holy Spirit is so vital for a believer to be spiritually alive that without Him, we are as good as dead. The Holy Spirit is truly like the very air we breathe.

> "Revival is contingent to the desire of the saints. Imagine what would happen if believers come together and pray persistently. We would see the power of the resurrected Christ."

4.    Waiting upon the Lord.

In the upper room, the 120 were waiting upon the Holy Spirit through prayer, worship, and supplications. They continued in one accord for ten days.

'All of these with their minds in full agreement devoted themselves steadfastly to prayer, [waiting together] with the women and Mary the mother of Jesus, and with His brothers' (Acts 1:14). By Acts 2:1-4 the Holy Spirit fell on all of them in a very dramatic way.

Today we can be filled the same way as in Acts 2. By doing what they did, we can experience what they experienced.

a.    All in one accord - this is dwelling together in unity.

"Behold, how good and how pleasant it is for brethren to dwell together in unity! It is like the precious ointment poured on the head, that ran down on the beard, even the beard of Aaron [the first high priest], that came down upon the collar and skirts of his garments [consecrating the whole body]. It is like the dew of [lofty] Mount Hermon and the dew that comes on the hills of Zion; for there the Lord has commanded the blessing, even life forevermore [upon the high and the lowly]' (Psalms 133:1-3).

There is so much power in unity that when two or more people come together in unity whatever they imagine doing, God will honor it. Whenever people are in one accord, there is an increase in authority in the realm of the Spirit. The greater the unity, the greater the authority. Psalms 133 says where people are in unity; God commands a blessing and even life for ever more. The power to birth things and bring forth life is found in unity.

b.    All in one place –

When people gather in one place, they consecrate the ground for the habitation of the Lord. Although God is omnipresent, His glory inhabits places where He is wanted. There is a need to create habitations of the Glory of God in our homes, churches, and communities. We need to know how to build altars in our homes, churches, schools, businesses and communities. The upper room was an altar consecrated in anticipation of the outpouring of the Holy Spirit. When people come together in one accord in one place, the power of unity increases in proportion. It releases greater authority in the spirit realm. That impact gets the attention of heaven. It is imperative that God must always respond to unity. He always goes to places where unity is exercised. Unity moves the attention of heaven in such a special way.

c.     They were in prayer and intercession -

God will never do anything in the earth until man prays. In 2 Chronicles 7:14 the Bible starts with the words

> 'if my people, who are called by my name, will humble themselves and pray and seek my face and turn from their wicked ways, then I will hear from heaven, and I will forgive their sin and will heal their land.'

Prayer is the condition set by God before He can hear from heaven and come down to heal the land. Jesus being the Son of God had no other way of talking to the Father except prayer. The secret of the mighty outpouring of the Holy Spirit that took place in the book of Acts was not just the fulfillment of the prophecy of Joel. Fulfillment of prophecy is not automatic. I submit to you that it was the answer to the prayer of unity that brought to pass the prophetic promises of God. Prayer prepares the way for the prophetic promises to be fulfilled. Even the birth of Jesus required the prayers of John the Baptist, Simon the elderly intercessor and Anna, the widow who lived in the temple.

In my years of study and walk with God I have concluded, that nothing moves until we pray. The upper room prayer meeting was going on day and night for ten straight days. Revival is contingent to the desire of the saints. Imagine what would happen if believers come together and pray persistently. We would see the power of the resurrected Christ. Revival happens when our desire for it leads us to a ceaseless pursuit of God. How bad do you want it? It is all up to you.

d.    They were in worship and supplication –

This is the aspect of drawing near to God in intimacy. Praise, worship, and supplication are like a magnet that attracts the presence of God. God inhabits the praises of His people. When we worship God, we experience the releasing of the Shekinah Glory. The tabernacle of Moses helps us understand a new and living way of worship. We can worship from afar or we can choose to draw near. That is why the tabernacle of Moses has three chambers; the outer court, the inner court and the Holy of Holies. Persistent worship creates a habitation for the Lord. It draws us near to worship, and we can experience His glory in the Holy of Holies. That is the chamber where the presence of God dwells with supernatural fire and the voice of the Lord. The upper room worship was so intimate and intense that it caused the Holy Spirit to come with a mighty sound from heaven and tongues as of fire. It is impossible to worship God this way and not experience the Holy Spirit in the same way.

e.   They had expectation –

There is evidence that over 500 people started out in the upper room on the first day. But by the tenth day, only 120 were left. The Holy Spirit will not come until He finds a high expectation. As long as there are unbelief and lack of expectation in the room, His presence will be delayed or limited. In this day and age, it becomes very challenging to build corporate expectation across different people and theological persuasions. In the upper room, all were filled not a few. All had cloven tongues as fire rested upon their heads and not a few. All spoke in tongues and not a few. There must be something they did differently that created this level of a breakthrough for all. I hope this breakdown helps you see the secrets of influencing heaven through prayer. The key word is "all." It means each and every single person was able to enter into the experience that was made available by the Holy Spirit.

The upper room experience was repeated in Acts 10. When Peter received a vision to visit the house of Cornelius and minister to the Gentiles, the Bible records what happened in verse 44.

'While Peter was still speaking these words, the Holy Spirit fell on all who were listening to the message.'

Peter was not able to lay hands on all of the people. The Holy Spirit went ahead of him and fell on the Gentiles.

In Acts 11:16 Peter explained that this experience reminded him of the upper room experience.

> 'Then I recalled the declaration of the Lord, how He said, John indeed baptized with water, but you shall be baptized with (be placed in, introduced into) the Holy Spirit.'

This encounter had a similar background with the upper room experience. Cornelius had taken the time to fast, pray and seek God. Peter as well was praying and fasting before the Lord sent him on this assignment. The people who gathered at Cornelius' house were in expectation. They took every word that Peter spoke as God's word for them. They simply created an atmosphere that attracted the Holy Spirit. If we build the right atmosphere, He will come.

There are other unconventional ways God fills people with the Holy Spirit. There are several people that have been baptized with the Holy Spirit during worship or personal prayer times. I have heard of several unconventional stories of baptism in the Holy Spirit. My wife is one of those. When I met her, she was not baptized in the Holy Spirit. My first date was held beside one of the 10,000 lakes in Minnesota. Our first thing to talk was on how to be baptized with the Holy Spirit. I shared what I knew, and then we left for the midweek service. During worship time, she was gloriously baptized with the Holy Spirit. She came to me crying and saying, "I got it, I got it!" I have heard of a man who was in desperate need of the Holy Ghost baptism. He woke up in the night to pray. In the process, he got so thirsty and opened the refrigerator to get a drink. The moment he touched it, he received the Holy Spirit. Others got baptized while in the shower. However, the key here is they were all very hungry.

I have also heard of a bizarre story where a mainline denomination pastor was preaching on baptism in the Holy Spirit. The elders did not like it when he began to pray for people. They did not want their church to begin speaking in tongues. One of the elders went to pull the pastor away and stop the ministration. Suddenly, he was struck by the power of God and began to speak in tongues. The other elders came quickly to control the situation. The first person to touch the pastor and the other elder also got struck by the power of God. They too began to speak in tongues. Such supernatural and unconventional means can also happen. Some churches and people need to be struck down by the love of God just like Saul on his way to Damascus. If the Lord chooses such a route, He is God. Let Him do it His way.

# CHAPTER 5.

# THE TANGIBLE EVIDENCE OF THE HOLY SPIRIT.

There are a lot of theological arguments on what being baptized with the Holy Spirit looks like. First of all, I would like to define key terminologies that I have been using throughout this book. I hope it is not too late to do this.

i)     The Holy Spirit versus the Holy Ghost

These two terms all refer to the same thing and can be used interchangeably. In my opinion, the term Holy Ghost raises more eyebrows than the term Holy Spirit. The use of the word "ghost" brings in a connotation of other spirits. There are many kinds of spirits, but there is only one Holy Spirit. There are many kinds of gods but only one God who is the creator of heaven and earth. In the same token, the

Holy Spirit is God, and He is distinct from other spirits because of His holiness. He is the HOLY Ghost. He is the "Ghost with the most."

ii)    Being filled with the Holy Spirit

To better understand this terminology we will use the example of a glass of water. It will stand for a vessel or a person. Every person who believes in Jesus Christ has the Holy Spirit. According to 1Cor 12:3

> "Therefore I want you to understand that no one speaking under the power and influence of the [Holy] Spirit of God can [ever] say, Jesus be cursed! And no one can [really] say, Jesus is [my] Lord, except by and under the power and influence of the Holy Spirit.'

No one can say Jesus is Lord but by the Holy Spirit.

According to John 16:8 it is the Holy Spirit that convicts a sinner to repent.

> 'And when He comes, He will convict and convince the world and bring demonstration to it about sin and about righteousness (uprightness of heart and right standing with God) and about judgment.' Nobody can become a believer in Jesus Christ without the Holy Spirit. This makes me conclude that all believers have a measure of the Holy Spirit.

In his vision, Ezekiel experiences the waters coming out from under the sanctuary of God.

'then he, [my guide] brought me again to the door of the house [of the Lord--the temple], and behold, waters issued out from under the threshold of the temple toward the east, for the front of the temple was toward the east; and the waters came down from under, from the right side of the temple, on the south side of the altar. Then he brought me out by way of the north gate and led me around outside to the outer gate by the way that faces east, and behold, waters were running out on the right side. And when the man went on eastward with the measuring line in his hand, he measured a thousand cubits, and he caused me to pass through the waters, waters that were ankle-deep. Again he measured a thousand cubits and caused me to pass through the waters, waters that reached to the knees. Again he measured a thousand cubits and caused me to pass through the waters, waters that reached to the loins. Afterward, he measured a thousand, and it was a river that I could not pass through, for the waters had risen, waters to swim in, a river that could not be passed over or through' (Ezekiel 47:1-5).

These waters symbolize the Holy Spirit. He also saw different levels of that water. These levels symbolize different dimensions of spiritual depth in our walk with God. Every born again believer has the Holy Spirit, but as the above scriptures indicate, there are different spiritual levels and dimensions. Ezekiel saw four levels:

a.    Ankle deep level -

This was very shallow waters that went only ankle deep. At this level, a vessel has very little influence and in-filling of the Holy Spirit. Such a person is not completely yielded to the Holy Spirit. Their flesh, will, and soul are still heavily dominated by the self. Such a believer struggles with being led by the Spirit because his flesh is still on the way. Though they are saved and can go to heaven, their life on earth lacks fruit, fulfillment, and victory. This is because the Holy Spirit has very little influence on their lives. In Romans 7:18-19 this kind of a person is called a carnal believer (one that constantly fails because they are ruled and dominated by the flesh)

'For I know that nothing good dwells within me, that is, in my flesh. I can will what is right, but I cannot perform it. [I have the intention and urge to do what is right, but no power to carry it out.] For I fail to practice the good deeds I desire to do, but the evil deeds that I do not desire to do are what I am [ever] doing.'

They have a desire to do what is right, but they lack the power to live a victorious Christian life. Through consecration and yielding, they can move up to the knee-deep level.

b.    Knee deep level -

Ezekiel saw this level but never described it in detail. However, at that level, he could not swim in the river. A believer with a knee-deep level of influence and infilling of the

Holy Spirit is not fully yielded to the Lord. God is calling us to die to the power of the flesh. If you look at the natural man, it is possible to continue living even after losing both feet all the way to the knee. This tells me that fleshly natural man has his will and desire still alive at the knee deep level. However, there is a higher level of yielding to the Holy Spirit that can lead them on to the waist deep level.

c. Waist deep level -

Here again, just like the other levels, Ezekiel's vision does not show the man overwhelmed completely by the waters. It is important to know that there are higher heights and deeper depths with God. We should never settle to die in shallow waters. The way to deeper levels is to have a higher influence and infilling of the Holy Spirit. Such a believer has a lot of passion and fruit and even gifts of the Holy Spirit at work. But they are not yet considered full of the Holy Spirit.

*"there are higher heights and deeper depths with God. We should never settle to die in shallow waters."*

d. Overflow level -

At this level, it is impossible for a person to be in full control. The waters are so deep that they have to swim. Swimming requires cooperation with the currents of the water. At this level, the Holy Spirit is in control. The vessel is considered fully yielded to the Holy Spirit.

Back to the analogy of water in a glass; a vessel can be full of water and even overflow but not be baptized. So what does it mean to be baptized with the Holy Spirit?

iii)   Being baptized with the Holy Spirit

The word baptized from a root word baptizo which means fully immersed under a liquid. This word was used to describe the act of dying a garment. It had to be fully immersed under the liquid for it to be considered dyed. A vessel can be filled to overflowing but can only be considered baptized if it is fully immersed under the liquid. Baptism in the Holy Spirit refers to being fully immersed under the Holy Spirit. The best way to describe this is through the story of Noah and the flood. The earth was baptized with water as God opened the sky and rained from heaven and the waters from the fountains of the deep gushed out because God caused the belly of the earth to open. The Holy Spirit wants to fall upon us and also out of our belly that the fountains of the deep would open and rivers of living water would flow. He wants us to be totally saturated by the Holy Spirit. Paul describes this in Ephesians 3:19.

> '[That you may really come] to know [practically, through experience for yourselves] the love of Christ, which far surpasses mere knowledge [without experience]; that you may be filled [through all your being] unto all the fullness of God [may have the richest

measure of the divine Presence, and become a body wholly filled and flooded with God Himself]!'

It is impossible to be filled with all the fullness of God without being baptized with the Holy Spirit. God desires for us to operate at this level. Are you ready to move up higher and deeper? Past generations have done it. Our forefathers in the faith did it. If they could get there, why not us and why not now?

After the 1904 Azusa Street revival, there was the re-birth of the Pentecostal movement. Many Pentecostal preachers birthed new churches that emphasized on the baptism in the Holy Spirit. There were so many arguments on what it truly meant to be filled and baptized with the Holy Spirit. Some churches claimed to have the new Pentecostal experience even though they lacked some of the evidence of it. Even to this day, there is still many Christians who claim to have the Holy Spirit baptism even though their lives show no evidence of it. It is sad to say that many churches and believers continue with their religious motions, without any idea that the Holy Spirit is no longer present. Without an understanding of the tangible evidence of the Holy Spirit, there is no way of telling when He is there or when He has departed. If we don't know where we are going, how shall we know when we get there? It is sad to say that many people are so used to doing things their way and never working with the Holy Spirit. Whenever we adopt that kind of a style, we will wake up one day and continue with business as usual without knowing that the Holy Spirit has departed.

## HERE ARE SOME INTERESTING OBSERVATIONS.

*The initial evidence vs. the consequential evidence.*

During the Azusa Street revival, the Pentecostal fathers coined the term "initial evidence." Under that term, nobody was considered to be filled or baptized with the Holy Spirit if they lacked the initial evidence of speaking in tongues. The purpose of this book is to take us past the initial evidence. I would like to add that it is possible to have the initial evidence and lack the consequential evidence of the Holy Spirit. I have met many people who are stuck with the initial evidence of speaking in tongues but do not have any other evidence that the Holy Spirit is working in them. This is like getting into someone's house only to get stuck in the threshold. The Lord has invited us into a relationship that has deeper depth and intimacy. He wants us to go to the deepest chambers of His presence. The initial evidence is just a doorway to a very deep and vital relationship with the Holy Spirit. Gaining access to different rooms of a house depends on the level of relationship you have with the owner of that house. Visitors are allowed to some rooms in the house, but only the bride and the groom are allowed to dwell in the most intimate chamber in the house. God has called us to be the bride. In my time of prayer and study, I have concluded that there is more evidence of the Holy Spirit beyond the initial evidence. This book has no intention of taking away from what has been laid by our spiritual forefathers. But we have to understand that revelation expands. God can reveal more truth to build on what was already set on the foundation. That is why I submit to you that we should move beyond the initial evidence and explore all other evidence and then make a wholesome conclusion.

Jesus in Mark 16:17 said that all believers shall speak with new tongues.

> 'And these attesting signs will accompany those who believe: in My name they will drive out demons; they will speak in new languages;'

In Acts 2:1-4 all of the 120 were filled and baptized with the Holy Spirit and spoke in tongues. In Acts 10:44 - 46 the Gentiles received the Holy Spirit and were heard speaking with tongues and magnifying God. In Acts 19:6 all the believers in Ephesus received the Holy Spirit and spoke in other tongues.

> 'And as Paul laid his hands upon them, the Holy Spirit came on them; and they spoke in [foreign, unknown] tongues (languages) and prophesied.'

It is very consistent in the book of Acts, in the early church, nobody was considered to have received the baptism and infilling of Holy Spirit without this initial evidence of speaking in others tongues. It is like someone selling hotdogs. Although it is advertised as hotdogs for sale, it goes without saying that every hotdog sold must be wrapped up in a bun. Anyone advertising sale of hotdogs and refuses to give the bun is considered a fraud. Sometimes we receive the baptism in the Holy Spirit, and all we get is the hotdog. It is just mere tongues. But we also need the bun. We need the power that wraps it all together. I have visited many churches and interacted with many preachers and Christians. I see the hotdog. But I always ask, where is the bun?

## Why tongues?

Tongues are important evidence which comes with incredible benefits. Jesus promised that all the believers shall speak in tongues. There are two types of tongues. There are those which are considered generic and are for all believers. Also, there those which are part of the nine gifts of the spirit and they require interpretation.

## Generic Tongues

There are several generic gifts in the Bible. For example, all believers have faith, but not all believers have the gift of faith. Faith is a generic gift and also a gift of the Spirit. All believers are called to be witnesses of Jesus Christ as evangelists. However, not all believers are in the office of an evangelist. Every believer can lay hands on the sick, and the sick will recover, but not all believers have been given the gift of healing. This clearly shows that most gifts of the Spirit have both the generic and specific version. The best example would be that most people in America drive, but not all are professional drivers. It takes a special license and qualifications to become a professional driver or to drive race cars. When it comes to tongues, I will focus on the generic tongues and not the gift of tongues that requires interpretation.

The ability to speak in generic tongues is the initial evidence that a believer has received the baptism in the Holy Spirit. In the book of Acts, nobody was considered baptized in the Holy Spirit without the evidence of speaking in tongues. Bear in mind that in Acts 1 and 2 when they were waiting for the Holy Spirit, they had no idea in what form the Holy Spirit would come. They did not have any preconceived ideas on what to expect but were totally open to the leading of the Holy Spirit. They knew Jesus in the flesh as a 33-year-old male wearing a long robe and a nice beard. The early church had no clue what form the Holy Ghost will appear in. I guess a mid aged bearded man would have shown up in the upper room and said that they are the Holy Ghost and everyone would have believed it. But the Holy Spirit showed up in a totally different manner. He came with one key initial evidence that was repeated again and again and again in the book of Acts. Please notice, in Acts 2, Acts 10 and Acts 19, only one evidence of speaking in tongues was consistent.

That is why it is called the initial evidence. In Acts 10, Peter affirms that this baptism was consistent with how it happened in Acts 2. He uses this argument in the Jerusalem Apostolic Council of the Gentiles, to validate the legitimacy of the move of God in the house of Cornelius.

This initial evidence was the sign that they have received the Holy Spirit. In Acts 10:44-46 Peter identifies speaking in tongues as the initial evidence to confirm the baptism of the Holy Spirit.

> 'While Peter was still speaking these words, the Holy Spirit fell on all who were listening to the message. And the believers from among the circumcised [the Jews] who came with Peter were surprised and amazed because the free gift of the Holy Spirit had been bestowed and poured out largely even on the Gentiles. For they heard them talking in [unknown] tongues (languages) and extolling and magnifying God. Then Peter asked.'

In his defense of what had happened in the house of Cornelius, Peter refers to the fact that they had been baptized with the Holy Spirit just like the 120 in the upper room.

> 'If then God gave to them the same Gift [equally] as He gave to us when we believed in (adhered to, trusted in, and relied on) the Lord Jesus Christ, who was I and what power or authority had I to interfere or hinder or forbid or withstand God?'(Acts 11:17).

In Acts 19:6 Paul laid hands on the believers in Ephesus, and the initial evidence was speaking in tongues.

> 'And as Paul laid his hands upon them, the Holy Spirit came on them; and they spoke in [foreign, unknown] tongues (languages) and prophesied.' I submit to you that this initial evidence has not changed. Although a lot of people believe they have the baptism of the Holy Spirit without the evidence of tongues, I will submit to you that they lack the benefits that come with the tongues. For that reason, they can not claim to have the same experience like in the book of Acts. I have never seen anybody who does not speak in tongues used by God in the power of the Holy Spirit in signs and wonders.

(Please note: Every believer in Jesus has the Holy Spirit whether they speak in tongues or not. However, only those who speak in tongues are considered to be baptized in the Holy Spirit)

There are several benefits that come with speaking in tongues. If I were on the other side of an argument that opposes tongues, it would be very difficult for me to be able to hold a position that denies people of these benefits. In fact, nobody who enjoys these benefits would like to see others denied of them.

## Benefits of tongues

i) Isaiah prophesied that tongues are for refreshment.

The amplified version talks of true rest, true comfort and happiness to the weary. This is the true refreshing. Speaking in tongues can reduce your stress level and refresh you physically and spiritually. Even a study that was done and reported by major respected newspapers and television news houses concludes that those who speak in tongues have less stress in their brain. That is because the brain/the mind is unfruitful/disengaged and only the Spirit is involved. Our bodies become the faculties that support the working of the Holy Spirit.

> 'No, but [the Lord will teach the rebels in a more humiliating way] by men with stammering lips and another tongue will He speak to this people [says Isaiah, and teach them His lessons] To these [complaining Jews the Lord] had said, This is the true rest [the way to true comfort and happiness] that you shall give to the weary, and, This is the [true] refreshing--, yet they would not listen [to His teaching]' (Isaiah 28:11-12)

ii) Praying in tongues is described as accurate prayer and according to the will of God.

The Holy Spirit prays on our behalf, and He prays according to the will of God. Everybody should have access to this benefit. We do not know how to pray. We need the Holy Spirit. There are times we do not have the scriptures to use in understanding of the will of God. We need to tap into the mind of God by praying in the spirit. For example, the only scriptural qualification/guidance on what kind of a person (of the opposite sex) to marry is not to be unequally yoked with an unbeliever. The Bible does not give any guidance on other aspects like age difference, race, economic differences, body type or educational gaps. When someone is praying for a mate, only the Holy Spirit can reveal the right believer to marry. Someone may be born again and meet the scriptural criteria for marriage, but may not be the will of God for a specific situation. Other times we do not know the scriptural way of praying for someone. By being led of the Spirit, He will pray for us according to God's word. Prayer in tongues will always be answered 100%. The Holy Spirit helps us to apply the word of God correctly in a specific situation. When it comes to marriage, according to the Bible, any believer can marry any eligible believer. But we all know not all eligible persons are a good fit for each other. To be able to find the right match and mate, we need the Holy Spirit to guide us. That's why I love praying in tongues.

> 'So too the [Holy] Spirit comes to our aid and bears us up in our weakness; for we do not know what prayer to offer nor how to offer it worthily as we ought, but the Spirit Himself goes to meet our supplication and pleads in our behalf with unspeakable yearning and groaning too deep for utterance. And He Who searches the hearts

of men knows what is in the mind of the [Holy] Spirit [what His intent is] because the Spirit intercedes and pleads [before God] in behalf of the saints according to and in harmony with God's will' (Roman 8:26-27).

iii)  Praying in tongues builds us in our most holy faith.

The Greek meaning of the word "building or edifying" has to do with laying a brick on top of another. It means to construct or build a house by laying a brick on top of another. I believe this is the same thing that the Bible calls the temple of the Holy Spirit. We are the temple of the Holy Spirit. The Bible describes us as living stones

'But you, beloved, build yourselves up [founded] on your most holy faith [make progress, rise like an edifice higher and higher], praying in the Holy Spirit;' (Jude 20).

Praying in the Holy Spirit is one way to grow into maturity and rise up higher and higher.

iv)  Praying in tongues fans into flames the gifts of the spirit.

It is one way of stirring up our spirit to allow the flow of spiritual gifts. There is a very strong connection between praying in tongues and the operation of the gifts of the Spirit. It is impossible to access the flow of the gifts of the Spirit without the ability to speak in tongues. Since the believers in the book of Acts believed in this initial evidence, it is no wonder that they experienced so much demonstration of the power of God.

## What about tongues as a gift of the Holy Spirit?

This is a specific gift listed among the 9 gifts of the Holy Spirit. It is a gift that brings forth the word of the Lord through tongues. It is not a prayer language but rather a message from the Lord to the believer that is delivered in tongues. 1 Cor 14 indicates that such a message must be interpreted in a known language. This gift must be handled with decency and protocol for the church to reap the full benefits of it.

There is no need to interpret the prayers in tongues or to forbid people from praying in tongues. The Bible clearly states that such a use of tongues (prayer) speaks to God and utters mysteries in the Spirit (1 Cor 14:2). However, the gift of tongues does not speak to God. It originates from the Lord speaking to men. This gift must be used alongside the gift of interpretion of tongues. In a nutshell, tongues spoken to God do not need interpretation. Of course, they are mysteries, and God understands all of that. But those tongues that God speakers to us through his vessels are mysteries that we need to understand. That is why they require interpretation.

2.    Love is the next evidence of the spirit of God.

In the book 1Cor 13, Paul elevates love as the highest evidence of the presence of the Holy Spirit. In verses 1-3 the evidence of love surpasses tongues, gifts of the Holy Spirit and good works.

> 'IF I [can] speak in the tongues of men and [even] of angels, but have not love (that reasoning, intentional, spiritual devotion such as is inspired by God's love for and in us), I am only a noisy gong or a clanging cymbal. And if I have prophetic powers (the gift of interpreting the divine will and purpose), and understand all the secret truths and mysteries and possess all knowledge, and if I have [sufficient] faith so that I can remove mountains, but have not love (God's love in me) I am nothing (a useless nobody).Even if I dole out all that I have [to the poor in providing] food, and if I surrender my body to be burned or in order that I may glory, but have not love (God's love in me), I gain nothing' (1Cor 13:1-3).

Speaking in tongues without love is empty, hollow and just a bunch of noise. The gift of prophecy that is able to access mystery and all knowledge is reduced to nothing without love. All good works, generosity and ultimate self-sacrifice are nothing without love. Even faith that can move mountains is considered nothing and of no profit without love. God is love. Anything devoid of love is not from God. Love is the only thing that bears the evidence of the presence of God. The revelation of love is the revelation of God. Without God, we are not able to understand love and how to love. We cannot give love if we do not have it in us. Love comes from God because He is love. God has love, but above all, He is love embodied in a person. That love was expressed by Jesus at the cross. He laid down His life for our sins.

When God's love is revealed in us, it enables us to love just like God. We are no longer restricted by our human weaknesses and limitations. That is why we are able to love our enemies and even those who despitefully use us. No matter what is said or done to us, the only way we can respond is with love. This kind of love cannot be based on our humanity. It is not based on a feeling. Jesus did not depend on feelings while on the cross. He anguished and suffered to death. It was love that held Him on the cross. Love has to be rooted in God. The ability to love like God and to demonstrate the love of God sets us apart from those who do not have the Spirit of God. Many people will be touched by that kind of love and will want to have what we have. Love becomes an evidence of how truly transformed we are. Love is the centerpiece and main fulcrum that holds everything together. Paul calls love a more excellent way. It is the more excellent way of bearing the evidence of the presence of the Holy Spirit. Love is not a product of our works. It cannot be produced through more efforts on our part or by observation of religious chores. Love is a gift from God. Romans 5:5 says,

"The love of God is shed abroad in our hearts by the Holy Spirit which is given unto us."

Love is given by God, but not expected of us to produce on our own. Without the Lord and the presence of the Holy Spirit, nobody can produce the love of God. That is why Gal 5:22 calls love the fruit of the spirit.

'But the fruit of the [Holy] Spirit [the work which His presence within accomplishes] is love, joy (gladness), peace, patience (an even temper, forbearance), kindness, goodness (benevolence), faithfulness.'

Perfect love casts out fear. Where fear is there is torment.

'There is no fear in love [dread does not exist], but full-grown (complete, perfect) love turns fear out of doors and expels every trace of terror! For fear brings with it the thought of punishment, and [so] he who is afraid has not reached the full maturity of love [is not yet grown into love's complete perfection]' (1John 4:18).

Faith also works with love.

'For [if we are] in Christ Jesus, neither circumcision nor uncircumcision counts for anything, but only faith activated and energized and expressed and working through love'(Gal 5:6).

It is very interesting to see what happens when love is withdrawn from something. When love is withdrawn from faith, faith fails. When love is withdrawn from the gifts of tongues, they become empty, hollow and a bunch of noise. When love is withdrawn from mercy, it gets compromised with the sin of tolerance. Love does not compromise with sin neither does it offer unsanctified mercy. Real love must have God as the object of our obsession. In so doing, that love is holy and pure. It is a love that hates sin. It is a love that seeks to please God. It is a love that focuses on what is in the heart of God. Such a love calls sin by its name and leads people to repentance other than tolerance. When the message of grace is preached without love, it becomes a grossly-greasy-grace.

Where there is no love, the Bible says there are fear and torment. In fact in 1 John 3:15 says that anyone who does not love his brother is called a murderer.

> 'Anyone who hates (abominates, detests) his brother [in Christ] is [at heart] a murderer, and you know that no murderer has eternal life abiding (persevering) within him.'

Those two scriptures suggest that in the absence of love there is fear, torment, and murder. This then points to a very serious conclusion. The absence of love is the absence of God because God is love. Also, the absence of God is the presence of Satan. It opens a door for him to bring fear, torment, and murder. Jesus made this conclusion: the world will know us as true disciples of Christ if we love one another.

'By this shall all [men] know that you are My disciples if you love one another [if you keep on showing love among yourselves]' (John13:35).

Nobody will deny the presence of the Holy Spirit in your life if you can love others. Everybody will want to have what we have. People can disagree with how you worship, how you pray, how you dance for God. They can call you weird or crazy. But if they find that you are full of the love of God expressed to others, they will want what you have. They will get more interested in the message we have if they see us live it.

If we truly have the Holy Spirit, it will show through our passionate love towards God, our neighbor, and ourselves. Let your love shine, and people will see it and glorify our Father in heaven. Love fulfills all the law and the prophets. It's the greatest commandment that sums all the others. Love is supreme. It is the ultimate evidence that the Holy Spirit is in and on us.

3.    Evidence of power

Jesus promised the disciples that they shall receive power after the Holy Spirit comes upon them.

'But you shall receive power (ability, efficiency, and might) when the Holy Spirit has come upon you, and you shall be My witnesses in Jerusalem and all Judea and Samaria and to the ends (the very bounds) of the earth' (Acts 1:8).

He also promised in John 14:12 that they shall do greater works than He did after the coming of the Holy Spirit.

'I assure you, most solemnly I tell you, if anyone steadfastly believes in Me, he will himself be able to do the things that I do; and he will do even greater things than these because I go to the Father.'

The presence of the Holy Spirit provides us with a unique ingredient that gives us a divine characteristic. The Holy Spirit releases a DNA in us which makes us full of the power of God. Ephesians 3:19-20 explains that as believers when we allow the Holy Spirit to come, we are filled with the fullness of God.

'[That you may really come] to know [practically, through experience for yourselves] the love of Christ, which far surpasses mere knowledge [without experience]; that you may be filled [through all your being] unto all the fullness of God [may have the richest measure of the divine Presence, and become a body wholly filled and flooded with God Himself]! Now to Him Who, by (in consequence of) the [action of His] power that is at work within us, is able to [carry out His purpose and] do superabundantly, far over and above all that we [dare] ask or think [infinitely beyond our highest prayers, desires, thoughts, hopes, or dreams].'

As a result, Christ in us can do exceedingly, abundantly above all that we can pray, think or imagine according to the power that is in us. This power is the ability to overcome all the powers of the enemy. The Holy Spirit gives power over sin, sickness, disease, poverty, perversion, and all kinds of demonic spirits. The same spirit that raised Jesus from the dead now resides in us. God never intended believers full of the Holy Spirit to live in defeat, especially in the face of sin, addictions, and satanic oppression. We have the same Holy Spirit that filled Jesus during His earthly life and ministry. The Holy Spirit gives us power to always triumph in victory. In the book of Acts, the group of the 120 did not come out of the upper room just talking in empty tongues. They walked out triumphantly in a demonstration of the power of God. They had no fear of death. They withstood persecution. They exercised power over sickness, disease, demons and death. They produced miracles, signs, and wonders. When the world saw the amount of power coming out through their ministry, they called them Christians. That was because they looked just like Christ.

Many years ago before I received the baptism in the Holy Spirit, I knew there was something I was missing. I was walking in a defeated life as a believer. The gifts of the Holy Spirit were not at work in my life. Although I loved the Lord, my prayer life was very weak. I was tormented by so much fear. I listened to a lot of teaching on the Holy Spirit. I heard about the many benefits of the Holy Spirit. I concluded that that was what I was missing. I began to seek God for the baptism in the Holy Spirit. The more I sought God, the more I had questions. I observed people who spoke in tongues and claimed to have the Holy Spirit and their lives were just as defeated as mine. I told God that when I receive the Holy Spirit, I would like to see the same things that happened in the book of Acts begin to happen in my life.

Prior to this experience as a university student, I was a member of a very powerful intercessory group. Some of our college mates had been used so mightily by God. One of the students was used by God to raise people from the dead. I had heard of others who moved in miraculous power over sickness and disease. I observed that all these students being used mightily of God had been filled with the Holy Spirit. I knew as soon as I got filled, I will be able to be used of God as well. One night I was waiting upon the Lord in a prayer meeting. On August 1, 1993 at 2am the Lord gloriously baptized me in the Holy Spirit. I had an encounter with the person of the Holy Spirit that left me gloriously transformed; never to be the same again. The Holy Spirit touched me and I fell and began to speak in other tongues. For three days in a row it felt like my mouth had been lubricated with oil and my tongue was sliding in my mouth. No matter what I was doing, I could feel the presence of the Holy Spirit on me. I was doing my finals at the college during that time.

The Holy Spirit was so strong in my life that even in the middle of the exams, I was still praying in tongues under my breath. My prayer life dramatically changed. I found myself praying longer and with more fire and life than before. In the past, I would run out of things to tell the Lord as soon as my list of prayer requests was done. After this experience, it became very clear that friendship with the Holy Spirit was more important than going to the Lord just to ask for stuff. I stopped treating God as an ATM machine and began to see Him as a friend. I saw the value of relationship, fellowship, friendship and communion. I found myself spending more time in worship and also praying for others. I quickly learnt the benefits of allowing the Holy Spirit to pray through us. He knows the best things for us and can pray them out according to the will of God.

When those changes took place in my life, within a few months of this encounter, I had a fulfillment of a dream of a lifetime. God miraculously connected me with my spiritual papa Dr. Morris Cerullo. The Lord granted me the opportunity to travel from Kenya to Uganda and attend the Morris Cerullo School of Ministry. I had an opportunity to be trained by Dr Cerullo and to be a part of God's Victorious Army that the Lord commanded Papa Cerullo to raise. He dealt with the question of 'What must I do that I might do the works of God.' During the teaching which he called 'The Journey to Power' I got a deep understanding of what it meant to move in the power of God. Dr. Morris Cerullo explained to us that with the presence of the Holy Spirit, we have what it takes to move in the power of God. At the final commencement of the school, there was to be the transfer of the anointing and an impartation service to all the graduates. That night I could not sleep. I knew there would be a transfer of the anointing and I had to prepare my heart for the release of the power of God. Then the day for the impartation came. The Holy Spirit fell in the room in a greater measure than I had seen before. Dr. Morris Cerullo asked us to lay hands on someone. When he released the impartation, the people I laid hands on were filled with the Holy Spirit and began to speak in tongues. For me that was a confirmation that I had received something I can give away. It took over 24 hours to get back to Kenya by train. I prayed in tongues the whole way. The Holy Spirit appeared to me several times on the way back with dreams, visions and heavenly encounters. I began taking notes of what He was saying. One of the instructions was to go back to Nairobi Kenya and preach on the baptism of the Holy Spirit. As soon as I arrived, I went straight to a meeting where I was asked to preach. I spoke on the baptism in the Holy Spirit. Immediately the power of God fell. People began receiving the Holy Spirit without hands being laid on them. It was such a powerful move of God being born.

Several months later, I met Dr. A.L. Gill. He taught me in another school of ministry on how to move in the power of healing. He explained again that all those things happened by the Holy Spirit. On the final night of the class, he anointed each one of us with oil. We were told to go and heal the sick. He also added we shall see people saved, healed, delivered and filled with the Holy Spirit. That night a group of us from the national university decided to take a bottle of oil to the National Hospital in Kenya. We took a bus and went straight to Ward number 13 where they housed people with liver problems. I found myself in a room with people who had swollen feet, and some of them could not walk. I did exactly what I had been taught to do. I led them to Christ, prayed for their healing, deliverance, and baptism in the Holy Spirit. To our amazement, we saw the same results over and over of people getting saved, healed, delivered, and filled with the Holy Spirit. They all spoke in tongues for the first time. The room was beginning to buzz with noise as people were getting touched by the power of God after being anointed with oil. Of course, I did not have a lot of wisdom or diplomacy because I was very excited about how God was using me. I had one of the relatives of someone we prayed for walk in the room just to see their loved one soaked with oil on the forehead and talking in tongues. The foot that was swollen was getting back to normal. They did not take what we were doing very kindly. They threatened to beat me up if

I didn't leave. I was all smiles as I walked out of the hospital. I knew I had the power of God on my life. I was so bold about it that no one could talk me out of it.

I got into the car and headed straight for my hometown. I took the platform to speak at a meeting organized by our university student Christian organization. Over 700 people had shown up. I spoke on the message of healing. I was so excited and fired up about it, I spoke with so much conviction and confidence that all the people knew that I knew what I was talking about. Although I was a young man with no title or church affiliation, the way I spoke with boldness made people believe in what I was saying. Right in the middle of the meeting, the Lord performed a public miracle. Since the meeting was outdoors in the marketplace, all the people could see what God was doing. Right before I started to preach, it began to rain. People ran for cover, and I knew if I didn't pray against the rain the meeting would be disrupted. I shouted into the microphone that we are going to stop the rain through prayer. Some people did not listen to my word. They just kept running. When I rebuked the storm and commanded the rain to cease, suddenly the Holy Spirit moved and swept the rain away from the meeting. Some still kept running away from the meeting because of the rains. However, the Lord caused the rain to clear from the crusade grounds. It kept on raining everywhere else except the crusade ground. For those running away, the only shelter was to come back to the crusade ground. God ensured that the meeting continued. Praise God that even the heavens could hear and respond to our prayer. I knew in my heart that the Lord would move mightily that night. We saw so many miracles. That was one of the signature crusades that started me off on my journey to the nations carrying the banner of Christ to multiple nations and continents.

This journey has taken me to stadiums, arenas, and churches around the world. I have seen the lame walk, the deaf hear, the blind see, demons leave, dead raised, thousands saved and filled with the Holy Spirit. I know despite all I have seen, the best is yet to come.

In the same year (1993), the Holy Spirit granted me the manifestation of the gifts of wisdom and word of knowledge. This was like being born again and again. To be saved is the greatest experience. But to be transformed this way by the Holy Spirit is a phenomenon experience! It expanded the boundaries of my ministry to being more than just about salvation, healing, and baptism in the Holy Spirit. God used these new gifts of the Spirit to give me access to the revelatory realm of power. It was through the gift of wisdom and word of knowledge that I got access to the ability to flow in prophetic ministry. Although this gift began manifesting by calling people out, it quickly evolved into the ability to speak prophetically into the lives of people.

That's what made 1994 one of the greatest years of my life in ministry. I was initiated into mass evangelism. It came through an aggressive evangelistic campaign that took me to most of all the major cities of Kenya. It was in this same year that the Lord took me to a certain community of destiny in Kenya. For over three months I lived and taught among them. Most nights would be spent in different homes and the weekends would be in different churches. Hundreds of people followed us everywhere we went. We would be in backyards of homes until 12 am in the morning. We had so many testimonies of deaf ears opening, blind eyes seeing, tumors disappearing, people being healed, delivered and baptized with the Holy Spirit. It was during this time that I saw thousands of peoples saved and transformed by the power of God. This was a further validation of my ministry through signs and wonders.

It was also in 1994 that the Holy Spirit appeared to me in a vision. I saw myself standing in a room that looked like a stadium. I was behind a pulpit in front of a crowd that I could not number. It was made of people of all colors and nationalities. I saw rain falling on them, and the voice of the Lord said go and participate in the revival. It was from that encounter that I got the name of my first ministry. The Latter Rain International Ministries came out of an interpretation of that vision. That was the year I knew that the Lord would send me to the nations of the world. I also knew that my call and ministry DNA shall be marked with the ability to reach people of different nations. Within two years of that vision, God had moved me from Africa to the United States. I was propelled and catapulted into an intercontinental ministry that I am still embarking on to this day.

There is so much power in the Holy Spirit. What God can do through the Holy Spirit is not dependent on our natural abilities but our availability. I had no natural endowments or major human relationships to rely on. I left Africa and came to America in full dependence on the Holy Spirit. This was my first time to get on an airplane. Everything was a miracle to me. It was a miracle to get an airplane ticket, passport, and a US visa. The US embassy required a minimum of $15,000 in the bank for one to qualify for a student visa to the United States. My bank statement had only $600. Yet, I was granted a visa. I believe it was the Holy Spirit that cleared the way and changed the rules of the game to get me through.

Although I came to America with only $200 in my pocket and a very vague knowledge of the western world, I held to the promise of what God had shown me in the vision. The things I have seen after the baptism in the Holy Spirit gives me the credibility to speak boldly of this one fact; that nobody can move in the power of God without the presence of the Holy Spirit. I arrived in New York with only $200 in

THE BOOK: THE TANGIBLE EVIDENCE OF THE HOLY SPIRIT | 119

my pocket and no clue on how to get from point A to B. During my flight, I prayed in tongues for many hours. The Holy Spirit assured me that everything would be all right.

Today, I have a testimony that looks like one of the great American stories. All things are possible through the power of the Holy Spirit. Since 1997 to this day I have seen the faithfulness of God. Without a work permit and income, the Lord sustained me. I had no money sent from Africa for my upkeep. I grew up in a very poor home. My father died when I was in the womb. My family would not have managed to send me support. But the Lord has a way of doing that which is impossible with man. The Holy Spirit can sustain us just like he did Elijah at the brook during the 3 ½ years of famine. All the years I have been in the United States, I have never been on welfare or dependent on food shelves. I have never been homeless or lacked in provision. I know that the Lord sustains those that are on His assignment. I managed to go to college and earn a master's degree in leadership. Although I enrolled without a student loan or a job, the Lord provided, and I was able to pay off the tuition fee in an unconventional way. Zechariah 4:6 is my story: It is not by might, not by power, but by the Holy Spirit. I have learned how to do everything by the Holy Spirit. Today God has put me on the frontline of a major ministry that is making an impact in the Twin Cities and around the world. He has blessed me with a family and kept me strong for the last days. Although I am not where I want to be yet, I am far ahead of what I used to be.

In the bible, nobody did anything powerful for God without the help of the Holy Spirit. God does not expect us to do anything by our might or power, but by the Holy Spirit. David, the shepherd boy, was enabled to become a king through the power of the Holy Spirit. When prophet Samuel poured oil on his head, the Spirit of the Lord came upon him. The assignment of Moses to deliver the children of Israel from Egypt was enabled by the Holy Spirit. God did not call Moses to fulfill a divine assignment without divine enablement. The encounter at the burning bush was a type of a Pentecost where Moses was baptized with the power of the Holy Spirit to go forth in signs, wonders, and miracles. That encounter was the secret behind his success. The children of Israel had been bound for 430 years. Moses made a daring move to embark on an impossible mission. But because he had been through the burning bush experience, he had the fire in the belly to fulfill the "mission impossible." Through the power of the Holy Spirit, mission impossible becomes mission possible. Even Jesus could not do any miraculous work until He received the experience of the Holy Spirit at the river Jordan.

'The [same] message which was proclaimed throughout all Judea, starting from Galilee after the baptism preached by John-- How God anointed and consecrated

Jesus of Nazareth with the [Holy] Spirit and with strength and ability and power; how He went about doing good and, in particular, curing all who were harassed and oppressed by [the power of] the devil, for God was with Him' (Act 10:37-38).

All the miracles of Jesus Christ were credited to the Holy Spirit.

'The Spirit of the Lord [is] upon Me, because He has anointed Me [the Anointed One, the Messiah] to preach the good news (the Gospel) to the poor; He has sent Me to announce release to the captives and recovery of sight to the blind, to send forth as delivered those who are oppressed [who are downtrodden, bruised, crushed, and broken down by calamity], To proclaim the accepted and acceptable year of the Lord [the day when salvation and the free favors of God profusely abound' (Luke 4:18-19).

The Bible makes it clear that it was the anointing of the Holy Spirit upon Jesus that destroyed the yokes and removed the burdens of sickness, disease, demons, and all the power of the enemy. Jesus did everything under the anointing of the Holy Spirit. All these miracles confirmed that He was Jesus the Christ. Since Christ is not His last name, we have to receive the revelation of the impact of the meaning of Christ. Christ is the anointed one; the Messiah; the one who comes to set the captives free. That anointing is the main evidence to prove the fact that Jesus is the one sent from heaven to set the people free. That is why Jesus could not fulfill His ministry without the power of the Holy Spirit. The Holy Spirit not only gave Jesus the credibility to minister but also enabled Him to produce the proof that He was who He claimed to be the Son of the living God. If Jesus, being God needed the Holy Spirit to do the works of God, how much more do we need Him today?

If we look at the life of Peter and the other notable men of God in the Bible, we see a similar trend. All their ministries started with a major encounter with the Holy Spirit. 'God will not use anybody until he gives them an experience,' (Morris Cerullo). Peter was a cursing-swearing-Jesus-denying-disciple. He was the hot-tempered son of thunder. He depended on his natural abilities and importance. When Jesus was being arrested, Peter drew out the sword and tried to defend Jesus with human strength. He chopped off the ear of Marcus, one of the soldiers who came to arrest Jesus. He was a natural man who did not understand the things of the Holy Spirit. When Jesus was arrested, crucified and buried, Peter forgot everything he had been told. Without the Holy Spirit, Peter could not remember that Jesus had promised that He would die and on the third day rise back up. Circumstances had become so overwhelming that it took only 72 hours for Peter and the disciples to lose the vision of who Jesus was to them. Within 72 hours Peter had lost the touch of God and had chosen to go back to his old life. He was a beaten down, backslidden man of God. Without the Holy Spirit, it is impossible to sustain the fire of God in our lives. When Peter came under fire, he lacked power because he did not have the Holy Spirit. To plow through the challenges of this walk of faith, we need to be propelled by the fire in the belly. The burden of the Lord is light. His yoke is easy. But it is only that way if we have the Holy Spirit working in the inside and showing in the outside.

When Jesus rose from the dead, He made it a priority to meet and restore Peter. He dealt with him in a very compassionate way. Jesus understood how hard it was for Peter. His spirit was willing to stand for Jesus, but his flesh was weak. Jesus offered him the opportunity to re-enter into frontline ministry under the power of the Holy Spirit.

He directed Peter and the disciples not to leave Jerusalem until they received the power of the Holy Spirit. In His own words Jesus concluded that after the Holy Spirit comes upon us we shall become His true witnesses. A witness is somebody who produces the proof of what they have seen and heard. Peter's ministry was set on fire after the baptism in the Holy Spirit. When he spoke, three thousand people were born again. Later on at the gate called beautiful, a crippled man was healed through his power-packed ministry. Under his leadership the church in Jerusalem grew in leaps and bounds. People were being added to the church every single day. Signs, wonders and miracles increased. People would lay the sick and demon possessed on the streets so that his shadow would heal them. When Dorcas died, it was Peter who went to raise her from the dead. Twice Peter was arrested and put in prison. The angel of the Lord broke the chains off Peter and opened the prison gates. Peter was unstoppable under the power of the Holy Spirit. This was not the same Peter who could not stand up for Jesus in front of a little girl. This was not the same Peter who had denied Jesus three times. This was not the same Peter who had gone back to his old life. This was a new Peter. He had encountered the Holy Spirit and was forever changed. He was now full of boldness in the face of persecution, death threats and government crackdown. The Holy Spirit had turned a spineless Peter into a bold witness for Jesus Christ. He was ready to preach and live for Christ and if necessary die. Peter died boldly and bravely for Jesus Christ. When he was arrested for execution, he requested to be crucified upside down. He wanted a more humiliating death than that of Jesus. Peter left a mark that can never be erased. No wonder, today we are here talking and writing about Peter. This could not have been possible without the Holy Spirit.

Time and space would not be enough to speak of people like Stephen, a man full of the Holy Spirit and faith. He was a deacon at the church in Jerusalem. A deacon with the Holy Spirit is more effective than a bishop without the Holy

Spirit. Stephen was full of signs and wonders. He was the first man to die for Jesus Christ. During his death that was witnessed by Paul, the heavens opened and he saw Jesus waiting for him. I believe that was the moment when Paul's life was impacted in preparation for his miraculous deliverance and release into ministry. Philip who was also a deacon at the church in Jerusalem moved in signs and wonders. He was a healing evangelist who is noted in the bible for the crusade he did in the city of Samaria. Multitudes received Christ and witnessed the demonstration of the power of God with healings and deliverances. The Bible says there was great joy in that city. Even Simon the sorcerer, who had set up a major demonic stronghold in the city, became born again. The Holy Spirit helped to open up an entire Gentile city for Jesus Christ.

We also read of Paul the apostle. After his conversion, he went to Ananias and received the Holy Spirit. The accomplishments of Paul's ministry are clearly documented in the book of Acts and the epistles of the New Testament. This high profile treatment of Paul's ministry has nothing to do with his natural abilities. Paul clearly says that he counted all his accomplishment as a loss for the knowledge of Jesus Christ. Paul gives us experiences of the greater works that we can do through Jesus Christ. These things can only happen by the Holy Spirit. Paul is the man that visited the third heaven. His encounters were beyond belief. He raised the dead. He brought the depth of wisdom and understanding of the things of God like no other person in this life. He listed and explained the gifts of the Spirit, the structure of the church and how to deal with issues in the church. He manifested a godly life for an earthly living. Even he said it in his own words, 'Imitate me as I imitate Christ". Today we look up to Paul as a major example of how a Christian should be. He raised the bar. He blazed the trail. He set the pace. He led the charge. He walked the walk and left a tangible evidence of the Holy Spirit. The mark that these men of God left cannot be erased. These are what I call the marks of the anointing.

4.  Evidence of fruit

Jesus said that you will know them by their fruit. Fruit does not lie. Like father like son. The root and the fruit are one. Out of the abundance of the heart, the mouth speaks. The fruit shows what is hidden in the heart. People can manage to hide things, but their fruit will tell on them. Where there is smoke, there is fire. Where there is the Holy Spirit, there is fruit. The Bible talks about the fruit of the spirit.

'But the fruit of the [Holy] Spirit [the work which His presence within accomplishes] is love, joy (gladness), peace, patience (an even temper, forbearance), kindness, goodness (benevolence), faithfulness, Gentleness (meekness, humility), self-control (self-restraint, continence). Against such things, there is no law [that can bring a charge]' (Gal 5:22-23).

Fruit grows, and it also glows. Fruit gets sweeter and riper. Fruit starts as a seed and increases in maturity. Any person with the Holy Spirit must show a consistent growth in the fruit of the spirit. This kind of growth is not a man made effort. Any fruit bearing tree produces effortlessly. It is not something a tree strives to produce. You will never see an apple tree striving to produce apples. They just appear naturally because of the fact that the core nature of the tree is an apple tree. The fruit is the evidence of the nature of who we are and what we have at the core. The ability to produce depends on being alive and in the right condition. We must also be in the right soil and feed off the right nutrients. Feeding right and being in the right condition is the key to producing the best fruit. As long as a believer is alive in the Spirit, the natural, effortless product of that relationship shall be evidenced by the bearing of the fruit of the spirit.

i)   Love:

The fruit that expresses selflessness. 1 Cor 13 explains what love is.

> "Love suffers long and is kind; love does not envy; love does not parade itself, is not puffed up; does not behave rudely, does not seek its own, is not provoked, thinks no evil; does not rejoice in iniquity, but rejoices in the

truth; bears all things, believes all things, hopes all things, endures all things. Love never fails." I Corinthians 13:4-8 NKJV

ii)    Joy:

The fruit of the overflowing presence of God that keeps us strong regardless of circumstances. It is not happiness or ecstasy. Happiness depends on the happenings. Joy is in spite of what is happening. Joy is as a result of a permanent state of overflowing presence of God. The joy of the Lord is our strength. Joy will keep you strong in all seasons.

iii)    Peace:

Peace is very elusive in the world. Peace that passes all human understanding is a fruit of the Spirit. It is possible to be at peace in the midst of unlikely outside circumstances. If there is peace in the inside, we can deal with the outside storms and still maintain our sanity. Jesus who is the prince of peace was able to sleep in a boat during a very harsh storm. Peace makes us to be unshakable even in times of storms of life. Peace is contagious. People who possess it are peace-makers.

Allow peace to become your umpire of your soul. Peace is the best way to discern the presence of the Holy Spirit. If I want to hear the voice of God, I normally ask him to manifest peace as the evidence. If I want to know the path I'm following, it's of the Lord, I want him to reveal it by showing me the evidence of his peace. Do you have peace about it?

It is one sign to know it is God. Where there's no peace, you feel a little striving and a sense of striving with doubt or an anxious check in your spirit. That's one way to know that God is restraining you from moving forward. You need to slow down and seek a direction that you feel peaceful about. Let peace be the umpire of your soul.

Paul puts it this way in his letter to the Philippians;

"Do not be anxious or worried about anything, but in everything [every circumstance and situation] by prayer and petition with thanksgiving, continue to make your [specific] requests known to God. And the peace of God [that peace which reassures the heart, that peace] which transcends all understanding, [that peace which] stands guard over your hearts and your minds in Christ Jesus [is yours]." PHILIPPIANS 4:6-7 AMP

iv)   Patience:

Long suffering is the other way to describe it. It is the fruit produced and enhanced by trials and refining fire of God. Apostles cannot get into their office without it. It is one of the key signs of the office of the apostle. It is love on trial. It is the ability to display love towards others and God in the most harsh circumstances. It is also the ability to trust the Lord in the midst of the most uncertain times. This fruit is developed in the trenches of the wilderness, the mountains, and valleys of life. Those who wait patiently on the Lord will be mighty in strength to mount soar up like eagles.

How are you responding to trials? How are you acting or reacting to rejection, family feuds, nagging mates, annoying workmates or a hostile working environment? What about that person that drives you nuts? Those are the trenches where you begin to develop your love walk. Do not run away from the opportunity to develop the fruit of long-suffering.

v)    Kindness:

It is the display of genuine, unfeigned love in public settings. It is the love of God displayed through tangible acts of kindness. God will anoint and fill your heart with the ability to do multiple random acts of kindness. They may be giving a smile, helping an elderly person, making a kind comment that is spoken without flattery. Allow God's kindness to flow through your words and actions. I remember a time I went to a restaurant with a friend. He is such a kind and generous man. We met two elderly women. They were probably in their mid-80s. I looked at them and said, "you are the cutest women I have ever seen." And I meant it! They smiled at me and said, "O how kind! You're the best. You made our day. Thank you". Then right after that, my friend walked right behind me and allowed one of the women to hold onto him. He walked her gently to her car. These were totally unrehearsed, unplanned random acts of kindness. They reveal Christ in us as God uses us as His hands and feet. Be kind. Sow kindness. The world needs to see our kindness. If we have a breakout of a revival of kindness, people would pick up trash, stop leaving gum on chairs, clean up after themselves, be gentle to the elderly, speak kindly to each other, pay debts and so forth. Marriages would be healed. People would reap what they have sowed.....kindness would beget more kindness. The world would begin to change one person at a time.

vi)   Goodness:

It is holiness on display. It is the revealing of the values and deposits that the Holy Spirit has put at the foundation of our hearts. It is the reflection of the goodness of God in our DNA. Goodness is the fragrance that makes us draw people to Christ as they are amazed by how good He is.

vii)   Faith: Utter unwavering trust in God.

Faith as a fruit is different from faith as a gift. It is possible to have the gift of faith that moves mountains and still lack the fruit of faith. Faith as a fruit works with love. Faith as a gift can work even without love.

(1 Cor 13:1, Gal). Nobody can please God without the fruit of faith. It is possible to have the gift of faith and not please God. Faith as a fruit is developed by exercising it like a muscle. The more you use faith in God the more it gets stronger. Faith in God is always a choice between God's way of doing things and other worldly ways of doing things. By constantly choosing God, we please Him, and our immovable faith in Him grows stronger.

viii) Gentleness:

It is controlled strength that brings glory to God. There is no glory for a 7ft, 200 Pound man being violent against a helpless 90-pound old lady. But there is great glory if that same person would use their great strength to save the little old lady from a violent gang. There is so much glory when we keep our strength under control and only release it when it is needed the most. Gentle people do not throw their strength around. Gentleness is also seen as meekness. It is the display of the character that helps us use our great strength with responsibility. The best example of this fruit is Jesus who is both the lion and the lamb. He knew when to tame the lion and only be the lamb. He never flexed His muscles or abused His power. That is why the power to rule the earth is in the hands of the meek. This power to rule and inherit the earth is so much and can only be entrusted to those who have the proven character to handle it well.

ix)   Self-control:

This is the ability to avoid excesses (even of good things) and other influences from taking over our lives. It is the ability to cultivate a balanced approach to life. It is the fruit of love of God where the self and its cravings are under total control. The appetites of the self are not able to take over in the life of a believer with self-control. This is the ability to keep spiritual sobriety in all aspects of our lives.

It is the fruit that allows a believer to tame, curtail and discipline the self to stay within the confines of the will of God. It is a life ruled by the Holy Spirit and not the self. Anybody aspiring to be a great leader in the last days must possess self-control. It is through this fruit that we shall be able to manage our personal desires and appetites. A successful leader does not over-indulge in a lavish lifestyle, sex, sleep, food, work or even hobbies. Self-control keeps a leader focused, balanced and sober-minded. The devil uses an area that is not under self-control as an open door for his temptations. Self-control keeps us from being vulnerable to the schemes of the enemy. Remember Samson, David, and Solomon. Their out-of-control lust and love for sex became their undoing. To Samson, Delilah was the tool the enemy used to crack through his incredible strength and reduce him to a mere vegetable. Everyone should ask for self-control to help seal the cracks in our armor. To somebody, Delilah is not a woman. It could be a man, food, computer, games or addictions that have developed and evolved into hardcore bondages. Self-control is what keeps us disciplined and free after being delivered. There is nothing more dangerous than a person who has lost control of the self. They are simply a loose canon. They are like a walking-talking disaster waiting to happen.

# CHAPTER 6

# THE SYMBOLS OF THE HOLY SPIRIT

1.    Fire-

Fire has different meanings in the Bible. There is the fire of judgment and destruction. The fire of hell and that of Sodom and Gomorrah were for destruction or judgment. The Holy Spirit is not for that purpose. The Holy Spirit is a refining-life-giving and passion-awakening fire. The book of Leviticus 6:12 says

> 'the fire on the altar shall be burning continuously and shall not be put out.'

The Holy Spirit is that fire. There are different references to the Holy Spirit as fire in the Bible

i)    He is the fire on the burning bush.

'Now Moses kept the flock of Jethro his father-in-law, the priest of Midian; and he led the flock to the back or west side of the wilderness and came to Horeb or Sinai, the mountain of God. The Angel of the Lord appeared to him in a flame of fire out of the midst of a bush, and he looked, and behold, the bush burned with fire, yet was not consumed. And Moses said, I will now turn aside and see this great sight, why the bush is not burned. And when the Lord saw that he turned aside to see, God called to him out of the midst of the bush and said, Moses, Moses! And he said, Here am I. God said, Do not come near; put your shoes off your feet, for the place on which you stand is holy ground. Also, He said, I am the God of your father, the God of Abraham, the God of Isaac, and the God of Jacob. And Moses hid his face, for he was afraid to look at God. And the Lord said, I have surely seen the affliction of My people who are in Egypt and have heard their cry because of their taskmasters and oppressors; for I know their sorrows and sufferings and trials. And I have come down to deliver them out of the hand and power of the Egyptians and to bring them up out of that land to a land good and large, a land flowing with milk and honey [a land of plenty]—to the place of the Canaanite, the Hittite, the Amorite, the Perizzite, the Hivite, and the Jebusite. Now behold, the cry of the Israelites has come to Me, and I have also seen how the Egyptians oppress them. Come now, therefore, and I will send you to Pharaoh, that you may bring forth My people, the Israelites, out of Egypt. And Moses said to God, Who am I, that I should go to Pharaoh and bring the Israelites out of Egypt? God said, I will surely be with you; and this shall be the sign to you that I have sent you: when you have brought the people out of Egypt, you shall serve God on this mountain [Horeb, or Sinai]. And Moses said to God, Behold, when I come to the Israelites and say to them, The God of your fathers has sent me to you, and they say to me, What is His name? What shall I say to them? And God said to Moses, I Am Who I Am and What I Am, and I Will Be What I Will Be; and He said, You shall say this to the Israelites: I Am has sent me to you! God also said to Moses, This shall you say to the Israelites: The Lord, the God of your fathers, of Abraham, of Isaac, and of Jacob, has sent me to you! This is My name forever, and by this name, I am to be remembered to all generations'(Exodus 3:1-15).

This fire is where Moses was transformed from being a fearful man without a vision into a man on a mission. His boldness, passion, tenacity and power to move in miracles was granted through the experience at the burning bush. This experience is necessary for each believer. This is the place where our journey to our destiny begins. Moses could not have confronted Pharaoh without this experience. He could not have overcome his low self-esteem and personal weaknesses without this fire. God can use anyone that has been baptized through fire. It was the turning point in the life of a man who had spent 40 years in the wilderness without a sense of direction. The final 40 years of his life became the most productive. The impact of his latter years superseded all his past 80 years combined. When the fire of God comes upon us, our latter shall be greater than the former.

ii)    He is the pillar of fire by night.

'The Lord went before them by day in a pillar of cloud to lead them along the way and by night in a pillar of fire to give them light, that they might travel by day and by night' (Exodus 13:21).

The Holy Spirit appeared to the children of Israel as a pillar of fire by night. He went ahead of them and sat over them. Whenever the pillar of fire moved, the children of Israel would dismantle their camp and follow the movement of the fire. They were being led by the Spirit. This fire also provided the light in their darkness. This underlines the importance of being led by the Spirit and walking in the light of God. It is not hard to follow the next season if we know how to follow the Holy Spirit. Transitions in life become more smooth and easy under the leadership of the Holy Spirit. The worst place to be is where God used to be but has moved on. Those are places of expired grace and old manna. Many people and churches keep functioning by the past experiences and what used to work. But we know that God is on the move. His Spirit is moving from one dimension to the other. We are constantly moving from faith to faith and glory to glory. God is releasing revelation knowledge to enable us to know how to follow the pillar of fire in our journey to destiny.

iii) He is the fire in the altar that consumes the sacrifice. His holy altar alters everything.

'The fire on the altar must be kept burning; it must not go out. Every morning the priest is to add firewood and arrange the burnt offering on the fire and burn the fat of the fellowship offerings on it.' (Leviticus 6:12).

It is the Holy Spirit that burns the sacrifice on the altar. Without Him, we will not be able to offer ourselves to God as a living sacrifice holy and acceptable to God, (Rom 12:1-2).

iv) He is the fragrance of worship that rises up to God like the smoke of the incense.

"And he shall put the incense upon the fire before the LORD, that the cloud of the incense may cover the mercy seat that is upon the testimony." (Leviticus 16:13)

v) He is the same fire that fell from heaven after the prayer of Elijah.

"Answer me, Lord, answer me, so these people will know that you, Lord, are God and that you are turning their hearts back again." Then the fire of the Lord fell and burned up the sacrifice, the wood, the stones and the soil, and also licked up the water in the trench. When all the people saw this, they fell prostrate and cried, "The Lord—he is God! The Lord—he is God!" (2 Kings 18:37-39).

Calling down fire from heaven enabled Elijah to show everybody that it is only through a living God that a distinction can be made between true and false worship. The presence of the Holy Spirit confirms that God is truly among us.

vi)    He is the Shekinah Glory in the Holy of Holies.

'Then there came a fire out from before the Lord and consumed the burnt offering and the fat on the altar; and when all the people saw it, they shouted and fell on their faces' (Leviticus 9:24).

This fire is the symbol of the divine presence of God. It is not the natural light of the sun nor the artificial fire of the candles. It is a supernatural flame of fire from the Lord. The divine presence of God is His dwelling place. It is the place of intimacy in worship and manifestation of the power of God. We must learn how to release this glory in our lives through worship and intimacy with God.

vii)     He is the fire that Jesus will baptize us with.

'I indeed to baptize you in (with) water because of repentance [that is, because of changing your minds for the better, heartily amending your ways, with abhorrence of your past sins]. But He Who is coming after me is mightier than I, Whose sandals I am not worthy or fit to take off or carry; He will baptize you with the Holy Spirit and with fire. His winnowing fan (shovel, fork) is in His hand, and He will thoroughly clear out and clean His threshing floor and gather and store His wheat in

His barn, but the chaff He will burn up with fire that cannot be put out'. (Matt 3:11-17).

The baptism with fire has different purposes:

a)    It refines our character.

Through trials and tribulation, our ability to endure to be patient and to wait upon God is tested. It is not enough to know God's word. We must be tested in the things we know and then proven. That is why every time God gives you a revelation, you will be tested in that area. It takes the fire of the Holy Spirit to have the character to live up to God's word. That which is not tested cannot be trusted. If your character is not tested, it cannot be trusted. God wants people on the frontline that have been tested through the fire. They are the proven vessels to carry the message of Jesus without fear, favor or compromise. They are dead men walking and cannot be intimidated even by death itself.

b)    It refines and purifies like gold.

The Bible calls it a refiner's fire Malachi 3:3 and 3:6.

"He will sit as a refiner and purifier of silver, and He will purify the priests, the sons of Levi, and refine them like gold and silver, that they may offer to the Lord offerings in righteousness. 'For I am the Lord, I do not change; that is why you, O sons of Jacob, are not consumed.'"

A refiner's fire does not destroy like a forest fire. It melts the gold and separates the impurities. The refiner's fire gets rid of the junk in our trunk. It targets the impurities, the chaff, and the dross. We are gold dug from the earth. Jesus redeemed us just as we are. The refiner's fire is the time and place where He purifies us to separate the gold from the impurities. When it is all done, we come out as pure as gold. Those who have been through the refiner's fire are able to walk in a higher dimension of purity than ever before. It is very critical that we submit to the process of being refined through the fire before we are elevated to higher dimensions. God wants us to be displayed on the platform of influence and mass impact. However, it is easy to get to the top without being tested. Gifts and special endowments can get anybody to the top. Unfortunately, many people have made it to the top without being qualified by character. They have displayed so many cracks in their foundation and shown a complete lack of integrity. As a result, they have shipwrecked and self-destructed while the whole world watches them humiliate themselves and the name of the God they claim to represent. Any minister with a vision to move in the high realm of impact and influence must allow the Lord to refine him in a real deep way. Always remember, the higher the building, the deeper the foundation.

c)     This fire will increase our passion for the Lord.

Being on fire for God is a "Christianese" (Christian lingo) term that simply refers to being very passionate about God. We become more passionate, loving and intimate with the Lord because of the changes we receive from our relationship with the Holy Spirit. A relationship in marriage or friendship needs fire to sustain it. Fire gives life to a marriage. It restores the spark of romance and sizzling of the relationship. It deepens the bonds of intimacy. If the spark is gone, the fire of the Holy Spirit brings it back. Fire is needed for that personal revival and awakening to prayer, holiness, service, the pursuit of God and love for others. Fire separates the real men of God from the boys. It separates the lukewarm from those who have true depth. Instead of asking where is the God of Elijah, we should join in the old cry of desperation and say, "Lord, send the fire! Send the fire today".

viii) He is the fire that quenched the fire in the book of Daniel 3:1-7.

'Nebuchadnezzar the king [caused to be] made an image of gold, whose height was sixty cubits or ninety feet and its breadth six cubits or nine feet. He set it up on the plain of Dura in the province of Babylon. Then Nebuchadnezzar the king sent to gather together the satraps, the deputies, the governors, the judges and chief stargazers, the treasurers, the counselors, the sheriffs and lawyers, and all the chief officials of the provinces to come to the dedication of the image which King Nebuchadnezzar had [caused to be] set up. Then the satraps, the deputies, the governors, the judges and chief stargazers, the treasurers, the counselors, the sheriffs and lawyers, and all the chief officials of the provinces were gathered together for the dedication of the image that King Nebuchadnezzar had set up, and they stood before the image that Nebuchadnezzar had set up. Then the herald cried aloud, You are commanded, O peoples, nations, and languages. That when you hear the sound of the horn, pipe, lyre, trigon, harp, dulcimer or bagpipe, and every kind of music, you are to fall down and worship the golden image that King Nebuchadnezzar has set up. And whoever does not fall down and worship shall that very hour be cast into the midst of a burning fiery furnace. Therefore, when all the peoples heard the sound of the horn, pipe, lyre, trigon, dulcimer or bagpipe, and every kind of music, all the peoples, nations, and languages fell down and worshiped the golden image that King Nebuchadnezzar had set up.'

The fire of the Holy Spirit quenches all the other false fires. When the enemy puts fire to destroy us, we can walk through that fire and not get burnt. Shadrach, Meshach, and Abednego showed by example that if we don't bow, we will not burn. When Nebuchadnezzar threatened them with a fiery furnace, the three Hebrew men knew that they had enough fire in them to take them through that fire. There are different false fires that threaten our lives. The lust of the flesh, anger, greed, and the threats of Satan are some of the things we have to deal with in our walk with God. If we do not bow to them, they will not burn us. The fire of the Holy Spirit in us is capable of quenching all those false fires.

ix)    He is the coal of fire that touched the mouth of Isaiah.

'Then flew one of the seraphim [heavenly beings] to me, having a live coal in his hand which he had taken with tongs from off the altar;' (Isaiah 6:6).

The coal of fire was from the altar which is the presence of God. This fire was for three purposes:

a)    For us to see the glory and holiness of God.

When the Holy Spirit comes, we see the holiness of God. When we stand in the presence of a holy God, we recognize our miserable-filthy condition. That is what made Isaiah fall on his face in repentance. Every revival must begin with conviction to repentance. God must be invited through repentance. The act of falling on our knees is not just for salvation. I remember in 1993 while conducting a revival meeting in the middle of the night. Prior to that night, I had not seen the level of glory that I saw. The power of God fell in the meeting like liquid fire. Crowds of people did not just fall under the power of God like a "curtsey drop" (where some people fall under the Spirit to impress the person laying hands on them). I am speaking of crowds of young men, old men, women, and children literally sliced off their feet by the power of God and swept off the floor like by a hurricane. When I saw it happen, I knew the Holy Spirit had come to take charge. I felt unworthy to lay hands on people. The ministry team and I fell on our faces and worshiped God in humility and repentance. As we were doing that, the people continued being touched miraculously by God's presence.

He is such a Holy God. When you see His glory come down, you too will be awestruck. Even John the Revelator who had been with Jesus multiple times had a similar experience. Although he had laid his head on His bosom and smelt His sweat, seen His blood and tears, none of those things compared to what he saw in the book of Revelation. When he saw Jesus in His glory and majesty, the Bible says he fell down as though dead. The glory of the Lord will cause us to no longer have that casual relationship that gets old and used to the move of God. We need another level of glory that will shake us up to the core. Even the angels in heaven cry out and bow before the Lord when they behold the ever increasing glory of God's holiness. They never get used to His presence. It is fresh and new every day.

b)    Cleansing-

The Holy Spirit comes as a consuming fire and cleanses our lives. No matter how long we have been with the Lord, we need a continual cleansing that is made possible through the Holy Spirit. Every new dimension must be ushered in through a new experience of cleansing. Therefore, the higher the calling, the greater the consecration. We must be ready to pay the price of a higher calling in God. The greater the calling, the greater the price of the consecration. Those who teach God's word are held into a higher requirement than anyone else. That is why they need the cleansing with the coal of fire to get rid of all the filthiness. God's servant must be above reproach. This fire removes the reproach.

"It is one thing for people to point out that you have a great calling on your life. It is another thing for you to see it, recognize it, respect it, expect it, step into it and pay the price for it. As Jesus said, many are called, but few are chosen."

c)    Calling-

Before stepping into the call of God in our lives, just like Isaiah, we need to be touched with a coal of fire in our mouths. It clarifies this dimension of calling in three different areas:

1)    The call -

This level clarifies that you are the man or the woman God has chosen to use and not another. It makes it very personal and gives you a reason to embrace the calling at a very personal and individual level. There will be no doubt ever that you are the called of the Lord. As a result, no one can confuse you or change your mind. This clarification also enables a person to believe in the anointing in their life. It gives you a new look at yourself. It is like looking at yourself in the mirror after an extreme makeover. You get to see the new you and embrace it. It is one thing for people to point out that you have a great calling on your life. It is another thing for you to see it, recognize it, respect it, expect it, step into it and pay the price for it. As Jesus said, many are called, but few are chosen. It is possible to find people with great callings on their lives who are wasting away in filthy lifestyles and meandering in the maze of mediocrity. This is because they have not attached a value on themselves and their calling. They need to be touched by a coal of fire so that they can believe in who they are in Christ and respect that calling.

After the fire has come on you, there will no longer be any doubts or second guessing on whether you are the one God wants to use. It is the first step towards getting sold-out for God. It, therefore, becomes easier to clean up the footlocker and get rid of the junk in the trunk. Whatever God would require of you, it is not hard to step into obedience.

2) The message –

This is the clear clarion call that will come out of your mouth. We are being sent with a very clear message. We must clarify our message so that we can clearly articulate it. The same God who calls is the same God who gives the message. The message for Moses was 'Let my people go.' The message for Jesus was 'To seek and to save that which was lost.' The message for John the Baptist was 'Prepare the way of the coming of the Lord.' I have been called to preach the message of healing and deliverance as well as equipping people for the work of the ministry. It is one thing to be called; it is another thing to know the message. Make sure you are called and also clarify what message God wants you to take.

These first two steps are like the first briefings of an ambassador who is being deployed on a mission. They need to be officially appointed and also briefed clearly on the role they will play. Never go ahead in your journey until you get down these two basic steps. Get briefed first. Receive your marching orders and then step out with utter abandonment.

3)    The mandate –

This level of clarification clears all confusion regarding the geographical location of your calling and the boundaries of your assignment. Moses was sent to a particular geographical location to take his message and given a certain measure of influence. He was careful to stay within the boundaries of his mandate. He did not overstep or overdo his assignment neither did he underperform. Many preachers have embarked on politics and other endeavors that are not within the boundaries of their mandate. While some have been mandated to be doing those things, not all are called for such expanded roles. God has called me to influence governments, public policy, marketplace, school systems, media, arts, and family. However, I have not been called to abandon my pulpit ministry and go into those endeavors. I have not been asked to shun but rather to shine in those dark places. By God's grace, I am called to mount a pulpit on all those spheres of influence by equipping, training and sending those whose lives I touch. By knowing your mandate, it is easy to stick to the vision and the mission. What did God tell you when you encountered Him? Did you get Him to touch you with the coal of fire? If not yet, let Him do it today. It will make your calling more precise and particular.

Peter was an apostle to the Jews. Paul was an apostle to the Gentiles. Jesus ministered only to the lost sheep of the house of Israel. We are not called to everybody. God has given people different realms of the rule. These realms of rule or territories can be expanded. We need to know and embrace the expansion of territory as granted by God. Jesus told the disciples to start from Jerusalem to Judea, Samaria, and expand to the uttermost parts of the earth. Their mandate continually expanded by the leading of the Holy Spirit. The more we are able to clarify our calling and all the specifics of it, the more effective we are going to become.

Every ambassador must clarify their appointment. Then they must know what message to take. They must also know what country or part of the world they are being called to serve. God's calling is not vague. Do you know your message? Do you know your geographical location? Before you depart, know your destination and the message you are to carry. Know the boundaries of your expansion in different seasons of life. Even a river knows its banks. An ocean with all its waters and soaring waves also knows its shorelines. Seek God for this. Don't be in a hurry to go. After all, where are you rushing to?

The coal of fire in the mouth of Isaiah is still available today by those who desire it.

    x)    The fire that fell on the day of Pentecost was the same on Mount Sinai and the upper room.

'Mount Sinai was covered with smoke because the Lord descended upon it in fire. The smoke billowed up from it like smoke from a furnace, and the whole mountain[a] trembled violently.' (Exodus 19:18).

'When the day of Pentecost came, they were all together in one place. Suddenly a sound like the blowing of a violent wind came from heaven and filled the whole house where they were sitting. They saw what seemed to be tongues of fire that separated and came to rest on each of them. All of them were filled with the Holy Spirit and began to speak in other tongues as the Spirit enabled them.' (Acts 2 1-4).

This fire was a sign of the presence of God. It is also a fire for empowerment. It is similar to the fire that is produced during the launch of a rocket on its way to the moon. It is a sign of the intense power of God that was released to birth the nation of Israel and the church. These two incidences of fire were at the birthing of two major moves of God. These two institutions are the nation of Israel and the church. Both were born with great power and in a demonstration of God's presence. They both have a very significant part in the destiny of the world. The church is the salt and light of the world. It is the only institution that makes the world a good place to live in. Without the church, this world will be like a hell on earth. On the other hand, the nation of Israel is a very small territory in the world. Its size is of almost no significance. But its influence surpasses most continents combined. There is no week that passes without Israel dominating the world news. As Israel goes, so goes the world. The calendar and thermometer of the changing times, seasons and dispensations are measured by looking at Israel. If you want to see what is about to happen, watch Israel and the church. That is why these two institutions were birthed with fire.

God wants you birthed with fire. It is critical we ensure that we are born into ministry right. Your entire life and ministry can be crippled by complications during the time of being born. God wants you to be launched right. He did it right with Israel. He also did it right with the church. He wants to do it right with you too.

xi)  The fire into which Paul shook the snake that bit his hand was the fire of the Holy Spirit.

"But Paul shook the snake off into the fire and suffered no ill effects' (Acts 28:5).

This fire is the presence of the Holy Spirit that destroys demonic power. As believers, we should be free to call on the fire of God and destroy demonic power. Anything that is holding on us, we can shake it off into the fire of the Holy Spirit. As a result, we shall not be harmed. The Holy Spirit destroys the power of the demonic forces. I have had the honor of calling down the fire from heaven many times in prayer. Sometimes the atmosphere is so tense and full of depression and heaviness. Through fire prayers, we can set out the flame of God's presence to clear the atmosphere and burn away the cloud of heaviness. (I have included some fire prayers at the end of the book).

2.   Water –

The different characteristics of water make it a very natural sign of the Holy Spirit. Water is a source of life just like the Holy Spirit. It is also fluid just like the Holy Spirit. Water also moves downstream and not upstream. The Holy Spirit moves in a direction where there is no striving. Water quenches thirst in the natural just like the Holy Spirit quenches our spiritual thirst. Water is also used for cleaning and washing our body. The Holy Spirit is a cleansing stream of living water. This concept of water can also imply to rain as well as a river. God opens the heavens and water pour out as rain. God also causes water to rush through the land as a river. There are several references in the bible to water, rain, and rivers.

a)    Water –

The Holy Spirit was the water that came out of the rock in the wilderness. Jesus is the rock. The Holy Spirit is the water.

> 'I will stand there before you by the rock at Horeb. Strike the rock, and water will come out of it for the people to drink." So Moses did this in the sight of the elders of Israel' (Exodus 17:6).

This picture repeats itself again when we see Jesus on the cross. When they pierced His side, blood and water came out of his body. The church was birthed out of the pierced side of our Lord and Savior Jesus. Just like Eve (a type of the church), was birthed out of the side of Adam, so was the church birthed out of the side of Jesus. What a beautiful picture as painted by John!

> 'Instead, one of the soldiers pierced Jesus' side with a spear, bringing a sudden flow of blood and water.' (John 19:34).

He is the rock that produced the water of the Holy Spirit. That is why He said;

> 'Whoever believes in me, as Scripture has said, rivers of living water will flow from within them. By this, he meant the Spirit, whom those who believed in him were later to

receive. Up to that time, the Spirit had not been given since Jesus had not yet been glorified' (John 7:38-39).

Jesus himself, interpreted those waters coming out of our belly as the Holy Spirit. Jesus also told the woman at the well that He would give her living water and she would never thirst again.

"Jesus answered her, If you had only known and had recognized God's gift and Who this is that is saying to you, Give Me a drink, you would have asked Him [instead], and He would have given you living water. She said to Him, Sir, You have nothing to draw with [no drawing bucket] and the well is deep; how then can You provide living water? [Where do You get Your living water?] Are You greater than and superior to our ancestor Jacob, who gave us this well and who used to drink from it himself, and his sons and his cattle also? Jesus answered her, All who drink of this water will be thirsty again. But whoever takes a drink of the water that I will give him shall never, no never, be thirsty anymore. But the water that I will give him shall become a spring of water welling up (flowing, bubbling) [continually] within him unto (into, for) eternal life. The woman said to Him, Sir, give me this water, so that I may never get thirsty nor have to come [continually all the way] here to draw.' (John 4:10-15).

This water again is the Holy Spirit. He is the one who fulfills all the longings of our soul. Through Him, we are complete and shall not want.

In Ezekiel 47 the Holy Spirit is the water that came out from the sanctuary of the Lord. This water was for healing and restoration of the land. It brought forth an abundance of fish, trees, and fruit for food and healing. Everywhere these waters went, there was healing. These are the very key characteristics of the impact of the Holy Spirit.

I John 5:8 clearly states that,

'There are three that bear witness on the earth: the Spirit, the water and the blood and these three agree.'

The spirit and the water refer to God as the Spirit and the water as the Holy Spirit of God.

In Isaiah 44:3 this is a reference to the outpouring of the Holy Spirit in the earth.

'For I will pour water upon him who is thirsty, and floods upon the dry ground. I will pour My Spirit upon your offspring, and My blessing upon your descendants.'

b)    Rain -

It is produced when vapor goes up and condenses into water. The clouds gather to form rain and then it is poured out back to the earth. In places where there is a lot of vaporization, it rains more regularly (sometimes every day). This is also true to the outpouring of rain in the Spirit realm. When we send prayers and worship up to God, it comes back to shower the earth with the rain of the presence of God. The abundance of rain is connected to the abundance of food.

Whenever there is no rain, famine ravages the land. Elijah prayed for rain to end three and a half years of famine. He heard a sound of the abundance of rain.

> 'And Elijah said to Ahab, Go up, eat and drink, for there is the sound of abundance of rain' (1Kings 18:41).

I prophesy over you that your season of famine is over. The drought is over. It is time for an abundance of rain. God is causing the former seasons of disappointments to end. God also says He is moving you from the season of just enough to a season of more than enough. It is going to rain miracles, healing, family restoration, financial restoration and abundance in Jesus name. Receive and begin seeing this word fulfilled in every area of your life. In Jesus name; Amen.

In the days of Elijah, it rained right after the destruction of the four hundred prophets of Baal. It was primarily because people had turned back to God in repentance and recognition that the God of Elijah is the true God. This rain is the outpouring of the Holy Spirit that will come to the church when we fully turn to God in prayer and repentance. Just like Elijah did, we have to take the same measures. He destroyed the worship of Baal. He also repaired the altar and called on the name of the Lord. As a result, the Lord brought down an abundance of rain. Revival is always contingent on the hunger and the desperation of the people. Elijah recognized the importance of casting down the idols and false worship. God will always respond to true worship. He is looking for true worshipers who can worship Him in spirit and in truth.

> 'A time will come, however, indeed it is already here when the true (genuine) worshipers will worship the Father in spirit and in truth (reality); for the Father is seeking just such people as these as His worshipers' (John 4:23).

Secondly, we have to repair the altar to bring back holiness to the altar and restore our relationship with God in the secret places. And finally, we have to call on the name of the Lord, and He will answer with an abundance of rain.

The Bible talks of the former rain and the latter rain.

> 'And if you will diligently heed My commandments which I command you this day—to love the Lord your God and to serve Him with all your [mind and] heart and with your entire being—I will give the rain for your land in its season, the early rain and the latter rain, that you may gather in your grain, your new wine, and your oil' (Deut 11:13-14).

The former rain is between the months of October and December and is just before the planting season. This rain softens the ground in preparation for planting. The latter rain is between the months of March and April and is just before the harvest. It prepares the crops to mature in readiness for the harvest. The former rain is for establishing and restoring the church. There is so much that needs to be restored. The gifts, anointing, power, influence, and affluence of the church have to be restored. None of those things are possible without a mighty outpouring of the Holy Spirit.

The latter rain is for beautification and perfection of the church. Jesus is coming for a church that is beautified and glorified. It will have no spots or wrinkles. The messy condition of the church today is going to be changed through the outpouring of the latter rain. The church shall be glorious again. The glorification is a state of the display of the splendor of the Lord in our lives. This is the realm where the wealth, health, and condition of the church will become the envy of people of the world. The working of the supernatural power of God in our lives will cause the world to envy the church. It will also provoke the jealousy of Israel. That is what will influence Israel to receive Jesus Christ as their true Messiah. Many people in the world will not believe in the Bible as God's word. But if they see the believers transformed by God's word, they will want what we have!

c)    River –

In Isaiah 41:18-20 God says

'I will open rivers on the bare heights, and fountains in the midst of the valleys; I will make the wilderness a pool of water, and the dry land springs of water. I will plant in the wilderness the cedar, the acacia, the myrtle, and the wild olive; I will set the cypress in the desert, the plane [tree] and the pine [tree] together, That men may see and know and consider and understand together that the hand of the Lord has done this, that the Holy One of Israel has created it.'

This is about the Holy Spirit. It is the concept of the life-giving power of the Holy Spirit.

Also, the river of Ezekiel 47 as we saw earlier is the Holy Spirit. The river Jordan in the Bible has repeatedly been used to symbolize crossing over from one state of being to another. The ability to cross over in that sense can only be by the power of the Holy Spirit. In three situations the river Jordan provides this impact of the Holy Spirit. In the book of Joshua 4:1-4 the children of Israel crossed over the river Jordan. It symbolized the end of 40 years of being in the wilderness to the beginning of inheriting the land of promise.

'When all the nation had fully passed over the Jordan, the Lord said to Joshua, Take twelve men from among the people, one man out of every tribe, And command them, Take twelve stones out of the midst of the Jordan from the place where the priests' feet stood firm; carry them over with you and leave them at the place where you lodge tonight. Then Joshua called the twelve men of the Israelites whom he had appointed, a man from each tribe.' (Joshua 4:1-4)

It is the Holy Spirit that enables us to make such a transition. Elijah released the double portion of anointing to Elisha after crossing the river Jordan.

> 'When the Lord was about to take Elijah up to heaven by a whirlwind, Elijah and Elisha were going from Gilgal. And Elijah said to Elisha, Tarry here, I pray you, for the Lord has sent me to Bethel. But Elisha replied, As the Lord lives and as your soul lives, I will not leave you. So they went down to Bethel. The prophets' sons who were at Bethel came to Elisha and said, Do you know that the Lord will take your master away from you today? He said, Yes, I know it; hold your peace. Elijah said to him, Elisha, tarry here, I pray you, for the Lord has sent me to Jericho. But he said, As the Lord lives and as your soul lives, I will not leave you. So they came to Jericho' (2 Kings 2:1-4).

The Jordan River is the place of transition. To children of Israel, to Elijah and to Jesus, Jordan was a place of crossing over. The river Jordan is where mantles are transferred from one generation to another. Jesus was also baptized by John at the River Jordan. That baptism was very important for Jesus to launch his ministry (Acts 10:37-38)

When Jesus was thirty years old, He reached the age of maturity to enter into priesthood. As it was the custom of the Law of Moses, He had to be washed in water. Even the Holy Spirit confirms this major transaction of anointing. God spoke with an audible voice, and the Holy Spirit descended on Jesus in the form of a dove. John was able to pass down the mantle of ministry to Jesus at the river Jordan. This river is the place where the old generations and the new emerging generations meet to pass on the baton. The river Jordan symbolized a spiritual rite of passage into a higher calling in God. It is a place of crossing over.

Get ready. The Lord desires to have you cross over to the new season. Jordan must open. You must pass from your season of wilderness to the season of entering and inheriting the promises of God. We have a promised land that the Lord desires of us to enter. I sense the Lord is provoking a great transition in your life by the Holy Spirit.

3.   Oil –

The Holy Spirit is also symbolized by oil. The nature of the oil gives it characteristics that describe the characteristics of the Holy Spirit. Anointing oil has special fragrance. This represents the sweet smelling aroma of the Holy Spirit that pleases God. Also, oil is used to light candles and lamps. The Holy Spirit is the fire in our belly. He lights a fire in our lives to cause us to burn with his passion and love. He is the oil that causes us to burn for God. With fresh oil in our lamps, we can continue to burn brighter without burning out.

Oil also flows. The ability to flow helps it to permeate into different parts of our lives. Such a flow also lubricates our lives to eliminate friction. When the oil is flowing, there is less friction, less resistance, less strife and a better flow. God wants your marriage and family to be free from friction. He wants to end the friction in your business and your financial wellbeing. He wants you to get into the flow. There is a special anointing for family, finances, ministry, favor and anything you need in your life. That anointing eliminates strife and brings you into the flow of the blessing of the Lord. That blessing (ability to prosper and abound) is as a result of the anointing. Because of the blessing, sorrow is removed (strife and friction). Even your enemies begin to bless you. God causes your cup to overflowing with oil and shows favor even in front of your enemies.

Pure anointing oil is also good for the healing of skin ailments. Shepherds in the days of old would carry anointing oil to help to administer on the cuts, wounds, and breaches of their animals. The anointing oil was like one stop cure for skin rash, wounds and protection from infections. No wonder we anoint the sick with oil. It is not the oil that heals. It is the presence of the Holy Spirit through the administration of oil that causes the healing to take place.

In the Bible, oil was used to anoint and consecrate kings, priests, and prophets into office. It symbolized consecration into office by the outpouring of the Holy Spirit on their lives. The presence of the oil meant that the Holy Spirit was resting on the person. Nobody was allowed to occupy any of these offices unless they were anointed with oil. May the eternal oil of Zion fall on your life. May that anointing heals and consecrate you for your destiny.

In Exodus 40 the anointing was used in consecrating the tabernacle of Moses. God required that all the articles and furniture be consecrated with oil.

> 'And it shall be in that day that the burden of [the Assyrian] shall depart from your shoulders, and his yoke from your neck. The yoke shall be destroyed because of fatness [which prevents it from going around your neck]' (Isaiah 10:27).

It is the anointing that destroys the yoke and removes the burden. Oil in this sense symbolizes the delivering power of God. The anointing has unique ingredients with a divine characteristic that produces power over all the powers of the enemy. The ingredients in the anointing oil were supposed to be made in a specific way for them to produce the specific result that God intended.

The anointing oil was made from a mixture of different components that produced a perfume that pleased God. There were four spices that were used: liquid myrrh, sweet-smelling cinnamon, cassia and olive oil. This oil was never supposed to be replicated or used outside what is considered holy unto the Lord.

'Moreover, the Lord said to Moses, Take the best spices: of liquid myrrh 500 shekels, of the sweet-scented cinnamon half as much, 250 shekels, of fragrant calamus 250 shekels, And of cassia 500 shekels, regarding the sanctuary shekel, and of olive oil a hin. And you shall make of these a holy anointing oil, a perfume compounded after the art of the perfumer; it shall be a sacred anointing oil. And you shall anoint the Tent of Meeting with it, and the ark of the Testimony, And the [showbread] table and all its utensils, and the lampstand and its utensils, and the altar of incense, And the altar of burnt offering with all its utensils, and the laver [for cleansing] and its base. You shall sanctify (separate) them, that they may be most holy; whoever and whatever touches them must be holy (set apart to God). And you shall anoint Aaron and his sons and sanctify (separate) them, that they may minister to Me as priests. And say to the Israelites, This is a holy anointing oil [symbol of the Holy Spirit], sacred to Me alone throughout your generations. It shall not be poured upon a layman's body, nor shall you make any other like it in composition; it is holy, and you shall hold it sacred. Whoever compounds any like it or puts any of it upon an outsider shall be cut off from his people' (Exodus 30:22-33).

The anointing of the Holy Spirit is a unique ingredient with divine capabilities. It is holy and cannot be obtained outside the Lord. It is the power of God that destroys yokes and removes burdens.

4.    Dove –

A dove is a symbol of peace. It is also a symbol of the Holy Spirit in the Bible. In Genesis 8:11 the dove sent out by Noah is a symbol of the Holy Spirit sent out into the world from the presence of the Father. [In our previous writing we discussed this concept exhaustively]. During the baptism of Jesus, the Bible clearly states that the Holy Spirit fell on Jesus in the form of a dove.

> 'And when Jesus was baptized, He went up at once out of the water; and behold, the heavens were opened, and he [John] saw the Spirit of God descending like a dove and alighting on Him' (Matt 3:16).

The dove, unlike other birds, is not a scavenger. It is a non-aggressive bird that does not violently kill its prey. That is why it is a symbol of peace and humility. Also, doves are very very sensitive birds. They are so easy to scare away. When we understand the revelation of this symbol, it will help us to change the way we walk, talk or behave as carriers of the Holy Spirit. The Dove is no longer temporarily on us. This heavenly dove is in and on us. This Dove allows us to adjust our walk and begin to handle ourselves with more holy reverence, fear and trembling.

The humility of the dove is not to be mistaken for timidity. The Holy Spirit as well is non-violent and very peaceful. However, He is very strong and mighty in power. Jesus told His disciples to be as wise as a serpent but as harmless as a dove.

'Behold, I am sending you out like sheep in the midst of wolves; be wary and wise as serpents, and be innocent (harmless, guileless, and without falsity) as doves' (Matt 10:16).

It is through that attitude that they would gain strength over wolves. This is about the fruit of the Spirit. Although we may look harmless and humble, that is the very reason why we are strong and able to deal with wolves and serpents. With the Holy Spirit on our inside, we are simply very dangerous!

5.   Wind -

The Bible refers to the wind in two different settings.

The Wind can be destructive or constructive. Destructive wind is called a storm. Tornados and hurricanes come with strong winds. However, when the Holy Spirit comes like the wind, He brings in the flow of the presence of God.

'[You have called me a garden, she said] Oh, I pray that the [cold] [a]north wind and the [soft] south wind may blow upon my garden, that its spices may flow out [in abundance for you in whom my soul delights]. Let my beloved come into his garden and eat its choicest fruits' (Song of Solomon 4:16).

'The wind blows (breathes) where it wills, and though you hear its sound, yet you neither know where it comes from nor where it is going. So it is with everyone who is born of the Spirit' (John 3:8).

This reference to wind has to do with the manifestation of the movements of the Holy Spirit. During the day of Pentecost, on Mount Sinai and in the upper room there was the manifestation of a mighty rushing wind. This is in reference to the Holy Spirit. It is not unusual during times of worship to feel the wind blow in the room. Sometimes we have been in meetings where we feel the wind literally blowing heavily among us. Sometimes we have heard the noise of the strong wind. That again is to show the presence of the Holy Spirit.

6.  Wine –

The wine symbolizes the joy that comes from the presence of the Holy Spirit. The Bible uses the symbol of wine to refer to the Holy Spirit. In the book of Matt 9:14-17 Jesus uses the term old wine and new wine.

> 'And no one puts a piece of cloth that has not been shrunk on an old garment, for such a patch tears away from the garment and a worse rent (tear) is made. Neither is new wine put into old wineskins; for if it is, the skins burst and are torn in pieces, and the wine is spilled, and the skins are ruined. But new wine is put into fresh wineskins, and so both are preserved.'

The new wine means the fresh anointing of the Spirit. New wine is put into new wineskins. When a vessel is consecrated and set apart, the Lord pours in a fresh anointing of the Holy Spirit. The old wine is the old nature. It also includes the past spiritual experiences. The new wine is what God is doing in the now. In the story of Jesus at the wedding in Cana, He performed a miracle that provided the best wine. He kept the best wine for last.

This symbolizes that the glory of the latter house shall be greater than the former. During the day of Pentecost, the 120 were so full of the Holy Spirit that the people thought they were drunk with wine. They saw them talking like drunks and staggering under the power of the Holy Spirit.

Peter explained that they were not drunk with wine as everyone supposed. He admitted the fact that they were drunk but with something else other than wine. He defended the experience by saying it was only nine o'clock in the morning. It was not the right time to be drunk with wine. He explained that this phenomenon was the Holy Spirit as prophesied in the book of Joel 2:28.

The new wine provides joy, boldness, and refreshment. Paul encourages us not to be drunk with wine but to be filled with the spirit.

> 'And do not get drunk with wine, for that is debauchery; but ever be filled and stimulated with the [Holy] Spirit' (Eph 5:18).

The Holy Spirit is the real wine we are all looking for. He is the high we all want to get to. He is the real deal. Everything else is a counterfeit.

# CHAPTER 7

# PRAYING UNDER THE POWER OF THE HOLY SPIRIT

These are some powerful prayers that if you pray them every day, you will see the Lord visit you with answers like never before. Now that you understand the power of the Holy Spirit, it is time to unleash it through prayer.

## PRAYER FOR SALVATION.

Dear Lord Jesus, I am a sinner. I have sinned against you and others. I repent. I ask you to cleanse me with your blood. Make me your own. Write my name in the Lambs book of life. From this day forward, I receive my forgiveness. I turn fully to you. Satan, I renounce you. You are not my God. I will no longer listen to you. I belong to Jesus.

Jesus, I am all yours. I will live for you. I will serve you. All the days of my life are yours. So help me God.

## NOW THAT YOU ARE SAVED!

Thank you for making this powerful decision. Welcome to the family of God! Here are a few things to get you started:

i)   Read your bible. It is God's word for you. Let Him speak to you through His word.

ii)  Pray every day. Prayer is simply talking to God. Tell Him anything you want. Make him your best friend.

iii) Go to a good Bible-based church. This will be the way to get you growing in God's family at the local church.

iv)  Tell others what has happened to you. God has done so much for you to keep it to yourself. Confess Him to others, and He will confess you in heaven.

v)   Get baptized in water and in the Holy Spirit as well. That is where the power for victorious living comes from.

# PRAYER FOR THE BAPTISM WITH THE HOLY SPIRIT

Father, I come before you by faith. You promised to pour your Spirit upon all flesh. I am here to ask for the baptism in the Holy Spirit with the evidence of speaking in tongues. As a born again believer, this is a blood-bought promise. Holy Spirit come and enter into my life. Fill me to overflowing. I now open my mouth to speak in the new tongues as you give me utterances.

(Open your mouth, begin to speak in that strange language God gives you. Keep on worshipping and thanking God. He will continue to fill you to overflowing)

## PRAYER FOR A FRESH ANOINTING AND FIRE.

In the name of Jesus, I open my inside. For out of my belly shall flow rivers of living waters. Let the rivers flow. Let the fountains of the deep in me open. Let the heavens open over me. Fresh anointing and fire fall from heaven now. Burn the chaff and the dross. Awaken the mantles and anointing on me. Awaken the gifts and callings from me. Baptize me with your fresh anointing and fire. In the name of Jesus.

God of Elijah, hear my cry. Send the fire now. Saturate me with your glory and fire. Refresh my spirit. Rekindle the fire of prayer and fasting. Rekindle the passion to love you and to hate sin. Rekindle my commitment to you. Set me free from myself. Remove wrong people from my life by your fire. Put me in the right church. Put my passion to work only for you. Cut off the lust for other things. Let me burn for you. Let people come and watch me burn for you.

Father, In JESUS name, I ask for wisdom, knowledge, and understanding of Your Word.

Set my tongue on fire. Set my marriage on fire for you. Set my church, business, workplace, school, family, nation (add anything else), on fire for you. Awaken the sleeping giant in me. Anoint me in a new and a mighty way. In Jesus name. Amen.

(Written by Dr. Charles Karuku)

## PRAYER FOR YOUR PASTOR, YOUR LEADER, YOUR FAMILY, AND SELF.

Father, in the name of Jesus, I pray and confess that the Spirit of the Lord shall rest upon_____, the Spirit of wisdom and understanding, the Spirit of Counsel and might, the Spirit of Knowledge. I pray that as Your Spirit rests upon _____, they will make _____ of quick understanding because You, Lord, have anointed him/her to preach the Gospel to the meek, the poor, the wealthy, and the afflicted. You have sent _____ to bind up and heal the broken-hearted, to proclaim liberty to the physical and spiritual captives, and the opening of the prison and of the eyes to those who are bound.

_____ shall be called the priest of the Lord. People will speak of _____ as a minister of God, and he/she shall eat the wealth of the nations.

I pray and believe that no weapon formed against _____ shall proper and that any tongue that rises against _____ in judgment shall be shown to be in the wrong. I pray that you prosper _____ abundantly, Lord, spiritually, physically and financially.

I confess that _____ holds fast and follows the pattern of wholesome and sound teaching in all faith and love, which is for us in Christ Jesus.

_____ guards and keeps with the greatest love the precious and excellently adapted Truth, which has been entrusted to him/her by the Holy Spirit who makes His home in him/her.

Lord, I pray and believe that each and every day, freedom of utterance is given to _____ that he/she will open his/her mouth boldly and courageously as he/she ought to do to get the Gospel to the people. Thank you, Lord, for the added strength that comes superhumanly that you have given _____

I hereby confess that I shall stand behind _____ and under gird him/her in prayer. I will say only that good thing that will edify _____ I will not allow myself to judge _____ but will continue to intercede for _____ and speak and pray blessings upon _____ in the Name of Jesus Christ, Amen!

Scripture references: Isaiah 11:2,3 2 Timothy1: 13,14

Isaiah 61:1,6 Ephesians 6:19,20

Isaiah 54:17 1 Peter 3:12

# BIBLICAL AFFIRMATIONS TO DECREE OVER YOUR LIFE.

- My heart grows hot within me, and as I meditate, the fire burns; then I speak with my tongue.

- My tongue is the pen of a skillful writer. I write the words upon the tablet of my heart.

- My heart is stirred by a noble theme, as I recite my verses for the King.

- The Holy Spirit is my teacher and guide. He reveals the Word to me so that I can understand it.

- I have been enriched in all my knowledge and in all my speech.

- I do not put out the Spirit's fire. In fact, I fan into flame the gift of God, which is in me.

- I have the spirit of revelation and knowledge. I am coming to know Christ better every day.

- I have the glorious inheritance working inside of me.

- I have the same power of God that was used to raise Christ from the dead. I have resurrection power within me.

- I cast my cares upon the Lord because He cares for me and watches over me affectionately. He has my best interest at heart.

- I hunger for righteousness. I am filled with all the spiritual blessings in heavenly places.

- I meditate in the Word day and night so that I can recognize God's will and then act upon it. As I practice the Word, I am blessed in everything I do.

- I esteem my words and treat them with respect. More than that, I esteem God and His Word above everything.

- My words are increasing in power and force because I let nothing come out of my mouth except what is helpful in building up others according to their needs.

- I love my words. I reap my words. My words are working to produce life.

- The Spirit is turning up the power of my words because I speak God's words.

- God's Word is the final authority in my life. I do not accept anything that does not live up with God's Word.

- I reject all tradition that does not conform to God's Word.

- I refuse to say anything that would disrespect God's authority.

- I have a merry heart, and it does well like medicine.

- I am more than a conqueror through Christ who loves me.
- I have faith in my words. I believe what I say comes to pass.
- The Word is near me. It is in my mouth and in my heart. It is the word of faith that I proclaim.
- I have been created in God's image. I am a spirit, I have a soul, and I live in a body.
- God has given me dominion. I have the power and right to govern and control.
- My words are spirit, and they are life.
- My first job is to cooperate with God in naming the kind of life I will have.
- God's Word is not void of power. It has the ability within itself to reproduce. I make God's Word my words.
- I have been made complete in Him. I am growing up in my salvation. My faith is growing exceedingly.
- God is faithful. What He said, He is able to bring to pass.
- God's Word comes out of my mouth, and it accomplishes what God desires and achieves the purpose for which He sent it.
- I desire to please my heavenly Father by imitating Him.

- I will walk in love and walk by faith in God's Word.

- I do not go beyond God's Word. I speak not worldly words, but I speak godly words.

- Whatever is of a good report, I speak it and think it.

- My God shall supply all of my needs according to His riches in glory in Christ Jesus.

- He is my shepherd, so I don't have a care in the world.

- I can say what God has said. Because He has said, "Never will I leave you and never will I forsake you," I can say with boldness, "The Lord is my helper; I will not be afraid. What can man do to me?"

- All things are possible with God, and I choose to believe in Him.

- The world may trust in horses and chariots, but I trust in the name of the Lord.

- His name is a strong tower; I run to it and am safe.

- Like Mary, I receive God's Word into my heart, I meditate on it, and it becomes flesh.

- I will not speak what comes to my mind but will speak what is in God's mind.

- God's Word will not return to Him void but will accomplish what He desires and achieve the purpose for which He sent it.

- I plant the imperishable Word of God into my life and into others. It never fails to produce.

- I can trust in God's Word because it is impossible for God to lie. Let every man be a liar, and let God be true.

- I prophesy according to the measure of faith within me. I take God's Word and speak it out of my mouth before it happens.

- My faith comes by hearing as I listen to the Word of God.

- The hand of the Lord is upon me. As I prophesy, great things happen.

- I am a vessel for the Lord. He uses me as He sees fit. He is the potter, and I am the clay.

- Though the outward man is decaying, my inward man is being renewed day by day. My youth is renewed like the eagles. Like Moses, my eyes are not growing dim nor is my strength gone.

- I do not forget any of the Lord's benefits. He forgives all my iniquities, and He heals all my diseases. He satisfies my desires with good things. He redeems my life from the pit and crowns me with love and compassion.

- God works through my words.

- I release Christ in me, the hope of glory.

- I hear the sound of an abundance of blessings. It is coming my way! Glory be to God!

- I am a king. I reign in life through Jesus Christ.

- I am in charge of my life through God's power. I am not subject to the world's troubles.

- I am a priest and a king.

- I live by faith, not by sight. It doesn't matter what I feel like; I am a king.

- I reign in life through Jesus Christ.

- I rule over Satan and his cohort. I tread on serpents and scorpions. Nothing they try to do can harm me. I am under God's protection.

- I have the keys of the kingdom of God. What I bind, heaven binds. What I lose, heaven loses.

- I bind all forces of evil in my life. I lose all the blessings of God into my life.

- I put a guard over my mouth. I refuse to say anything wrong. I speak only God's Word.

- My body lines up to the words of my mouth. What I say is what I get. My body works perfectly, just the way God intended it to work.

- I don't verbalize my fears. I verbalize only my faith.

- It doesn't matter what trials come my way; I only speak what a good report is. The report of the Lord is I'm healed, I'm blessed, and I have victory through faith in Jesus Christ.

- I am raised up with Christ and made to sit with Him in heavenly places. I am on top of the world.

- I have no reason to fear the future. God has plans to prosper me and not harm me. He has plans to give me hope and future.

- I am following God's plan for my life.

- I know where I'm going because I have God's wisdom in my life. Jesus has given me wisdom from God.

- I am filled with good things by the fruit of my lips.

- Life and blessings are on my tongue. I speak only the good and not the bad.

- The life I am now living is the result of the words I spoke in the past. So, I am speaking good things now; later my life will become these good words.

- I will not walk in the negative words that people have spoken over my life. I bind those negative words from my life.

- I can do all things through Christ who strengthens me.

- I will live and not die, and I will declare the glory of the Lord.

- I am the world overcomer.
- Greater is the Holy Spirit who is in me than the devil who is in the world.
- All things work together for my good because I love God and are called according to His good purpose.
- Jesus bore the thorns to redeem me from the curse. I can produce fruit.
- I am a fruit-bearing branch of the vine of Jesus Christ.
- In Him I live, move, and have my being. I am a new creature in Christ Jesus.
- I am not going to let things happen to me. I am going to make things happen through my authority as a child of God.
- My success has nothing to do with luck or chance; it has to do with Jesus. He is my Lord! He is my boss.
- I am a new creature in Christ Jesus. The old me have died. The new me is full of joy, peace, and love.
- Angels protect me and encamp around me because I trust in the Lord.
- God is good and never brings tragedy into my life.
- I am blessed with all spiritual blessings in heavenly places in Christ Jesus.

- God has predestined me to be conformed to the image of His dear Son.
- I am adopted into God's family. I can call God, "Father."
- I am one of His chosen ones. He picked me for His family because He wanted to.
- God has set before me life and death. So, I choose life.
- There is now no condemnation for me because I am in Christ Jesus. I have chosen Christ because He has chosen me!
- I believe in divine healing.
- I receive healing according to my faith.
- Jesus heals all my diseases and sicknesses. He is still the same yesterday, today, and forever.
- I make Jesus my doctor and best physician.
- Surely, Jesus took up my infirmities and carried my sorrow. By His stripes I am healed.
- God is not the author of sickness and disease. Satan is the oppressor, and I resist Satan now.
- I forbid Satan to put any disease in my body. My body is the temple of the Holy Spirit.
- I resist all symptoms. I live by faith not by sight.
- I am in this world, but I am not of this world. I am delivered from this present evil world.
- A merry heart does well to me like medicine.

- The joy of the Lord is my strength. The glory of the Lord is my rearguard.

- God's Word is life and health unto all my flesh.

- Every part of my body functions perfectly. My eyes work well. My ears work well. My muscles work well. My heart works well. My bones work well. All my organs, tissues, cells, ligaments, hormones and blood work well.

- The Spirit that raised Christ from the dead is dwelling inside me and is making alive my mortal body.

- Jesus paid for my healing, so I'm walking in health.

- I know the grace of my Lord Jesus Christ. Though He was rich, yet for my sake, He became poor so that I could become rich.

- I am rich. I am abundantly supplied. I am highly effective. I am a success in every way.

- I use the power of God to meet any need. I do not lack any good thing.

- I am a seed of Abraham, so I am blessed along with him. I have his blessings. I walk in the blessings of Abraham.

- I remember the Lord, for it is He who gives me the ability to create wealth.

- I am blessed so that I can be a blessing.

- I refuse to allow the spirit of greed to control my life.
- I am a tither and give. I give, and it is given back to me in good measure, pressed down, shaken together, and running over.
- The Lord opens up the windows of heaven and pours out on me so many blessings that there is no room to contain. I overflow with blessings.
- The devil is rebuked from touching my finances.
- Christ has redeemed me from the curse of poverty, so I refuse to be poor.
- Poverty is underneath my feet.
- I am the head and not the tail. I lend unto many, but I do not have to borrow.
- I live under a better covenant, a covenant that has been ratified by the blood of Jesus.
- Jesus is the Guarantee of all the promises of God. He makes sure that I enjoy all my privileges and rights under the new agreement.
- I am the righteousness of God in Christ Jesus.
- I am growing in the grace of God. I am experiencing God's unmerited favor. I have favor with God and with men.
- People look upon me with kindness because I see people as my friends, not as enemies.

- I approach the throne of grace with boldness. I have a right to the Presence of God.

- I receive grace every time I ask for it. I ask, and I receive.

- I am as bold as a lion. I refuse to fear anything. I do not fear even when I hear bad news. My heart is fixed on trusting in the Lord.

- Wealth and riches are in my house.

- My faith may be tested, but I will pass the test.

- I inherit all the promises of God through faith and patience.

- I will not become bitter toward anyone, even if they slander me. I will pray for those who persecute me.

- I'm not afraid of the devil or his schemes. I have dominion over him.

- I fear not because God has not given me a spirit of fear, but of love, power, and a sound mind.

- Many are the afflictions of the righteous, but the Lord delivers me from them all.

- In this world, I shall have tribulations, but I am of good cheer because Christ has overcome the world.

- I am the world overcomer because I live by faith, not by sight.

- I have mountain-moving faith. I speak to mountains, and they obey me.
- I have Godlike faith. I believe; therefore, I speak. I have the spirit of faith. This faith overcomes obstacles.
- I put on God's fighting clothes. I put on the belt of truth. I have my feet covered with the preparation of the gospel of peace. I have my breastplate of righteousness in place. I put on the helmet of salvation and take up the sword of the Spirit, which is the Word of God. And above all else, I use the shield of faith to guard me against the arrows of the evil one.
- I am shielded by God's faith and power.
- I am a participant in the divine nature. I have God's faith, God's peace, God's joy, God's love, God's patience, and God's strength.
- I am regenerated. I have God's spiritual genes. If you've seen me, you've seen the Father. As Christ is, so am I in this world.
- I am growing up in my salvation. I have the joy of my salvation.
- My faith is growing exceedingly fast.
- I am learning to listen to God's voice and obey His Word.

- I refuse to say anything that I don't hear my Father saying. I speak only what I hear my Father speak.
- God has a wonderful plan for me. He plans to prosper me and not to harm me. He plans to give me hope and future.
- I trust God. I do not fear the future because God is in control of my life.

Adapted from Eagle Vision Ministry (Author UnKnown)

# ABOUT THE AUTHOR

D r. Charles is an apostle to the nations who has traveled around the world conducting healing and deliverance crusades since 1991. In stadiums, arenas, and churches, thousands have been saved and set free by the power of God. The lame walk, the blind see and the deaf hear as God's miraculous power is released to minister to the desperate needs of humanity.

As a speaker, author and trainer, Dr. Charles has traveled widely for seminars and conferences in leadership development and capacity building in over 23 nations in United States, Europe, South America, Asia, Australia, Canada, and Africa.

Dr. Charles is also an intercessor and a spiritual father whose main goal is to mentor people to help them fulfill their destiny in God. He is the lead pastor of International Outreach Church, a growing multi-faceted/multi-racial church in the Twin Cities MN, USA.

He is the President of the Institute of Leadership and Mentorship (ILM). He holds a Bachelors Degree in Education, a Master Degree in Leadership and two Honorary Doctorate Degrees in Humanities and International Relations. Dr. Charles is passionate about developing leaders and building capacity in organizations. He is an example of global leadership as he operates as a Golden Rule Goodwill Ambassador, a mentor, speaker, and leader.

Dr. Charles is a recipient of the prestigious Global Leadership Award as well as an appointed World Civility Ambassador.

He has produced numerous training materials and is also regularly heard in the State of Minnesota by live stream, media platforms, and training schools.

As a husband and a father of 5, Dr. Charles loves to coach soccer and inspire others. He enjoys watching documentaries and competitive sports games.

For more information, visit www.experienceioc.com, or www.ILMedu.com